# The 15-Minute
## JENNIFER LAMARR
# AIR FRYER
# COOKBOOK 2024
## FOR BEGINNERS

**BONUS**

Effortless Air Fryer Meal Prep for Health Enthusiasts

# 1800+ DAYS

of Super Easy, Tasty and Budget-Friendly, Low-fat, Air Fryer Recipes for Weight Loss & Eating Healthier. Tips for Perfect Frying and Baking

## NEW: SCAN QR, REVEAL RECIPES

# The 15-Minute Air Fryer Cookbook for Beginners

1800+ Days of Super Easy, Tasty and Budget-Friendly, Low-fat, Air Fryer Recipes for Weight Loss & Eating Healthier. Tips for Perfect Frying and Baking

by
**Ingrid Lamarr**

**Important Note for Readers:**
The recipes in this book are shared with the intent of offering culinary ideas and fostering a love for cooking. However, it is crucial to remember that each individual has unique nutritional needs, influenced by factors such as overall health, existing medical conditions, allergies, and personal preferences.
If you have serious health issues or are under medical treatment, we strongly encourage you to consult a doctor or a nutrition professional before making significant changes to your diet. Only an expert can provide advice on a personalized diet plan that takes into account your specific needs and health conditions.
This book aims to inspire and is by no means a substitute for qualified medical advice. Care for your health by making informed dietary choices and, when necessary, seeking the guidance of professionals.

# GET YOUR BONUSES NOW!

**Effortless Air Fryer Meal Prep For Health Enthusiast**

Download your free bonus meal prep guidebook now!

## Go to page 59 and download this amazing FREE BONUS.

## Sommario

Dear Reader,

We wish to share with you a fundamental decision we have made regarding the editions of our books, a choice driven by our commitment to sustainability and the preservation of our planet. Specifically, for our cookbook, we have implemented an innovation to improve its quality without compromising our environmental commitment.

We have chosen to print the physical copies of our books in black and white. This decision has been made with deep reflection and awareness, based on various key reasons related to environmental sustainability:

• **Ink Saving:** Black and white printing uses less ink, and the production of black ink is generally less environmentally impactful than that of colored inks.
• **Energy Efficiency**: Printers used for black and white production tend to consume less energy compared to color printers.
• **Waste Reduction**: By minimizing the use of multiple ink cartridges, we can reduce waste generated from expended cartridges.
• **Lower Costs**: Reduced costs of black and white printing allow for more economical and accessible production, with less environmental impact from production and distribution.
• **Sustainable Material Use**: We commit to using recycled paper or paper from sustainable sources, alongside eco-friendly printing practices.

To enrich our readers' experience without compromising these principles, for our cookbook, we have introduced a novelty: instead of including black and white images, each recipe is accompanied by a QR code. Scanning the QR code with a mobile device, readers will be able to view the color photos of the dishes. This approach not only keeps the physical book more sustainable but also enriches the reading experience with the vividness and visual appeal of the dishes in digital format.

We recognize the value and importance of your experience as a reader and want to ensure that, even as we adopt more ecological and sustainable measures, you do not miss out on the incredible world enclosed within the pages of our books, now enriched by an enhanced visual experience for our recipes.

Thank you for your ongoing support and understanding regarding this decision. Your passion for reading and your commitment to a more sustainable future make this community so special.

With gratitude and commitment towards a greener future,

Ingrid Lamarr

# Explore 1800 Days of Endless Culinary Possibilities

You might be wondering what "1800 days of recipes" means as highlighted on our book. This is not just a title, but a promise of variety and discovery. With an innovative approach, we transform a curated selection of recipes into a gastronomic adventure that accompanies you for a full 1800 days. Every combination of recipes is an opportunity to explore universes of flavors, textures, and pairings, turning the daily meal routine into an exciting culinary exploration.

Our book invites you to experiment and personalize your meals in constantly new and exciting ways, leveraging the versatility of the recipes to create an infinity of combinations. Cooking becomes a dynamic art, capable of offering new taste experiences every day. Each dish is seen not just as an end in itself but as a starting point for your creative explorations in the kitchen.

## Plan Your Meals with Ease

We've developed a system based on chapter and recipe numbers, allowing you to easily navigate through the book's pages and plan your meals with flexibility. For instance, the recipe "6.1" refers to the first recipe in chapter 6, while "7.3" indicates the third recipe in chapter 7.

## An Example of a Meal Plan

Here's how you might use our system for two days, keeping the example valid for any type of cookbook:
- **Day 1:**
    - Breakfast: Ch. 6, Recipe 1
    - Lunch: Ch. 7, Recipe 1 + Side: Ch. 16, Recipe 1
    - Dinner: Ch. 8, Recipe 1 + Side: Ch. 16, Recipe 2
- **Day 2:**
    - Breakfast: Ch. 6, Recipe 2
    - Lunch: Ch. 9, Recipe 1 + Side: Ch. 16, Recipe 3
    - Dinner: Ch. 7, Recipe 2 + Side: Ch. 16, Recipe 4

This model demonstrates how, by following our guide, you can create a varied and balanced meal plan, experimenting with new flavors and combinations. Our vision is for this book to become a valuable ally in your kitchen, stimulating the desire to explore and reinvent the pleasure of food. The promise of "1800 Days of Recipes" is to make the culinary art a continuous adventure, a journey of discovery and innovation.

# Lend Us Your Voice in Our Journey

As a publisher, every single review is fundamental support for us. Your voice can make a difference and help us continue our mission. If you believe in the value of what we do and want to lend us a hand, please take a moment to share your thoughts. Your review is our beacon in the vast sea of publishing. From the bottom of our hearts, thank you for your invaluable contribution!

Scan the Qr code with the camera of your mobile phone, click on the link that opens and you can leave your review. Thank you.

## https://bit.ly/airfryerkindlerev

# Introduction

The culinary world is constantly evolving, and one of the latest stars in the kitchen appliance galaxy is the Air Fryer. Resembling the functionality of deep frying, an Air Fryer harnesses the power of hot air to give food that tantalizing, crispy exterior without drenching them in oil. This revolutionary device is comprised of a heating element, a potent fan, and typically, a cooking basket or tray where you place your food. Once the device is activated, hot air circulates fervently, cooking your food to perfection and achieving that desired crispy finish.

One of the standout advantages of Air Fryers is their ability to reduce the oil quotient in your food. Traditional deep frying immerses food in copious amounts of oil, but with an Air Fryer, you get similar results using a mere fraction of the oil, championing a healthier cooking alternative.

Diversity is another strong suit of the Air Fryer. They are available in myriad sizes catering to different needs - be it for an individual or a bustling family. Their features too are nothing short of impressive. From the convenience of digital controls to the foresight of pre-set cooking programs and the precision of built-in timers, Air Fryers are a boon to the modern cook. To further sweeten the deal, some sophisticated models even offer added functionalities like pressure cooking or the ability to dehydrate food.

Delving deeper into the world of Air Fryers, this book is your definitive guide. Regardless of whether you're just beginning your Air Fryer journey or are an adept user, the contents herein promise to enrich your experience. We've curated an expansive range of recipes spanning breakfasts, lunches, dinners, and even decadent desserts. These dishes are not only a treat to the palate but cater to varied tastes and dietary inclinations. Be it the allure of crispy French fries, the succulence of perfectly cooked chicken breasts, or the crunch of garden-fresh vegetables, there's a recipe here for every craving. And for those with a sweet tooth, prepare to be amazed by desserts that your Air Fryer can whip up. Each culinary masterpiece is accompanied by detailed instructions and precise cooking times, ensuring you're well-equipped to recreate them in your kitchen.

# Chapter 1: Air Fryer Models

The popularity of Air Fryers has skyrocketed in recent times, giving rise to a plethora of models tailored to specific culinary needs and kitchen environments. As you delve deeper into the world of Air Fryers, it's essential to familiarize yourself with the diverse models available to make an informed choice.

## 1.1 Countertop Air Fryers

Arguably the most popular and widely recognized, Countertop Air Fryers are compact appliances designed to perch on your kitchen counter gracefully. Their size spectrum ranges from those ideal for individuals or couples to larger models that can cater to an entire family's crispy cravings. Irrespective of their size, these models retain the fundamental components: a heating element, a circulating fan, and a designated cooking area, often in the form of a basket or tray. Modern countertop models boast of sophisticated features like intuitive digital controls, preset culinary programs, and precise built-in timers for a seamless cooking experience.

## 1.2 Toaster Oven Air Fryers

This model ingeniously merges the functionalities of a traditional toaster oven with the unique capabilities of an air fryer. Naturally, given their dual-function nature, these are larger than your standard countertop variants. Beyond air frying, they lend themselves beautifully to baking, broiling, and toasting. Their enhanced capacity makes them a favorite among larger households or culinary enthusiasts who frequently entertain guests.

## 1.3 Multi-cooker Air Fryers

The epitome of kitchen convenience, Multi-cooker Air Fryers wear many hats. They consolidate the features of air fryers with other beloved kitchen mainstays like pressure cookers, slow cookers, and even dehydrators. Their multi-faceted nature makes them programmable to cater to a smorgasbord of dishes, from crispy fries to succulent slow-cooked meats and dried fruits.
They are the go-to choice for those who cherish versatility without cluttering their kitchen with multiple appliances.

## 1.4 Air Fryer Ovens

For those who desire the capabilities of an air fryer but on a grander scale, the Air Fryer Oven is the answer. These are substantial units, often comparable in size to traditional ovens, and can easily serve as their replacement. Their expansive interiors are equipped with additional features, such as integrated rotisseries, allowing users to roast meats evenly. Furthermore, they often come equipped with dehydration functions, making them a favorite among health enthusiasts keen on creating their own dried snacks.

In essence, with the myriad of models available, there's an Air Fryer tailored for every culinary need and kitchen space.

# Chapter 2: Tips for buying an Air Fryer

When buying an air fryer, there are a few things to consider so that you get the best model for your needs:

## 2.1 Size

Consider the size of your household and the amount of food you typically cook. Smaller, personal-size models are suitable for single or couple households, while larger, family-size models are suitable for larger families or for those who like to cook for guests.

## 2.2 Type

There are several types of air fryers available, such as countertop models, toaster oven air fryers, multi-cooker air fryers, and air fryer ovens. Consider which type of air fryer is best for you based on your cooking needs and the features you are looking for.

## 2.3 Capacity

Consider the capacity of the air fryer basket or tray. A larger capacity will allow you to cook more food at once, but it will also take up more space in your kitchen.

## 2.4 Features

Consider the features that are important to you, such as digital controls, preset cooking programs, a built-in timer, or additional functions such as pressure cooking or dehydrating.

## 2.5 Price

Air fryers come in a range of prices, from budget-friendly models to high-end models. Consider your budget and the features you are looking for when choosing a model.

Brand and reputation: Research the brand and reputation of the air fryer you are considering and read reviews and feedback from other customers.

## 2.6 Accessories

Some air fryers come with accessories such as drip trays, skewers, or rotisserie baskets. Consider if these accessories will be useful for your cooking needs.

## 2.7 Size and design

Be aware of the size and design of the air fryer. It should fit in the available space in your kitchen and match your kitchen design.

## 2.8 Ease of cleaning

Look for an air fryer that is easy to clean and maintain, with removable and dishwasher-safe parts and a self-cleaning function if possible.

## 2.9 Safety features

Look for an air fryer with safety features such as an automatic shut-off, overheat protection, and a cool-touch handle.

# Chapter 3: How To Clean An Air Fryer

Cleaning an air fryer is important to maintain its performance and to ensure that your food doesn't absorb any unwanted flavors or odors. Here are a few tips for cleaning your air fryer:

## 3.1 Unplug the air fryer

Make sure to unplug the air fryer before cleaning it.

## 3.2 Empty the basket or tray

Remove any food debris from the basket or tray and discard it.

## 3.3 Clean the basket or tray

The basket or tray can be washed in warm, soapy water or put in the dishwasher if it's dishwasher safe. Use a soft sponge or brush to clean it gently.

## 3.4 Clean the interior

Use a damp cloth or sponge to wipe down the interior of the air fryer, including the heating element and fan. You can use a mild detergent or a cleaning solution specifically designed for air fryers.

## 3.5 Dry the air fryer

Once you've finished cleaning the air fryer, make sure to dry it thoroughly before using it again.

## 3.6 Clean the outside

Use a damp cloth to wipe down the exterior of the air fryer.

## 3.7 Clean the accessories

If your air fryer comes with any accessories, such as a drip tray, skewers, or a rotisserie basket, make sure to clean those as well.

## 3.8 Check the manual

Always consult the manufacturer's manual for specific cleaning instructions and recommendations for your particular model.
It's recommended to clean your air fryer after each use to keep it in good working condition and to ensure that your food doesn't absorb any unwanted flavors or odors. Some air fryers also have a self-cleaning function; you can check if your model has this feature and follow the instructions provided.

# Chapter 4: Tips and Tricks

## 4.1 Preheat the air fryer before cooking

Heating up the air fryer ensures that the food is cooked consistently. It also helps to create a crispy exterior on the food. Most air fryers have a preheat function, or you can preheat it by setting the temperature to the desired level for about 3-5 minutes before adding the food.

## 4.2 Use less oil

Air fryers are designed to cook food with less oil than traditional deep frying methods. You can use as little as a tablespoon of oil for most foods or none at all for some foods.

## 4.3 Use a cooking spray or oil mister

To ensure that the food doesn't stick to the air fryer basket or tray, you can use a cooking spray or oil sprayer to lightly coat the food.

## 4.4 Shake the basket or tray occasionally

To ensure that the food cooks evenly, shake the basket or tray occasionally during cooking. This helps to redistribute the hot air and prevent hot spots.

## 4.5 Don't overcrowd the basket or tray

Overcrowding the basket or tray can prevent hot air from circulating properly, resulting in uneven cooking. Make sure to give the food enough space so hot air can circulate around it.

## 4.6 Use parchment paper or aluminum foil

To prevent food from sticking to the basket or tray, you can line it with parchment paper or aluminum foil. This also makes it easier to clean the air fryer.

## 4.7 Cut food into uniform pieces

Cutting food into uniform pieces helps to ensure that it cooks evenly.

## 4.8 Use a meat thermometer

To ensure that your food is cooked to the desired level of doneness, use a meat thermometer to check the internal temperature.

## 4.9 Cook food in batches

If you're cooking a large amount of food, it may be necessary to cook it in batches to ensure that it cooks evenly.

Experiment with different cooking times and temperatures: Different foods may require different cooking times and temperatures to achieve the desired level of doneness. Experiment with different settings to find the best ones for your food.

## 4.10 Use the air fryer's accessories

Some air fryers come with accessories such as a drip tray, skewers, or a rotisserie basket. These accessories can be used to cook a wide variety of foods, so be sure to take advantage of them.

## 4.11 Let the food rest

Once the food is cooked, let it rest for a few minutes before serving. This allows the food to finish cooking and redistribute its juices.

## 4.12 Use a timer

Most air fryers come with a built-in timer, or you can use a separate timer to keep track of the cooking time.

## 4.13 Clean the air fryer regularly

To keep your air fryer in good working condition clean it regularly, according to the manufacturer's instructions.

---

**Image Disclaimer:**
Please note that the images contained within this publication are for illustrative purposes only. They are intended to provide a visual reference and may not accurately represent the final appearance of the recipes. Variations in ingredients, cooking methods, and individual execution can result in differences from the depicted images. We encourage creativity and personalization in your cooking, allowing room for interpretation and adaptation based on your preferences and available ingredients.

# How to Use the QR Code to See Photos of the Recipes

Hello! Do you want to see beautiful, colorful photos of the recipes you're reading in the book? Just follow these easy steps. It's as simple as playing a game!

1. **Find the QR Code**: Flip through the book until you find a recipe you like. Near the recipe, you'll see a little square filled with black and white dots. This is called a "QR Code".
2. **Use your mobile phone**: Grab your smartphone or tablet. Yes, the very one you use to call friends or play games!
3. **Open the camera**: Tap the camera icon on your device's screen to open it, just like when you want to take a picture.
4. **Aim at the QR Code**: Point the camera at the QR Code in the book. You don't need to press or touch anything, just hold the device steady and make sure the QR Code is clearly visible on the camera's screen.
5. **Click on the Link**: After a little while, you'll see a link (a line that starts with "http://" or "https://") appear on your phone's screen. Tap this link with your finger.
6. **View the Photo**: Wait a moment and... ta-da! The colorful photo of the recipe will appear on your phone's screen. Now you can see exactly what the finished dish should look like!

Remember: if you're having trouble, ask for help from someone younger or a friend. It's a fun activity to do together, and soon it'll be a piece of cake!

# Chapter 5: Breakfast Recipes

## 5.1 Apple Fritters

These Apple Fritters are a delightful treat, combining the sweetness of apples with a hint of cinnamon, all wrapped in a light and crispy batter. Chosen for its simplicity and deliciousness, this recipe is perfect for a cozy breakfast or a sweet snack.

**PREPARATION TIME:** 10 minutes
**COOKING TIME:** 8 minutes
**DIFFICULTY LEVEL:** Easy
**SERVINGS:** 2

**INGREDIENTS**
1. Cooking spray
2. All-purpose flour, 1/2 cup
3. Ground cinnamon, 1/2 tsp
4. Granulated sugar, 1/4 cup
5. Lemon juice, 1 tbsp
6. Salt, 1/2 tsp
7. Eggs, 2
8. Baking powder, 2 tsp
9. Milk, 2/3 cup
10. Honeycrisp apples, 2, thinly sliced
11. Butter, 1/4 cup
12. Confectioners' sugar, 1 cup
13. Vanilla extract, 1 1/2 tsp

**STEPS**
1. Preheat the air fryer to 410°F.
2. In a large mixing bowl, combine flour, baking powder, salt, cinnamon, and granulated sugar. Add milk, lemon juice, 1 teaspoon vanilla extract, and eggs, stirring until the mixture is moist. Fold in the sliced apples.

3. Scoop 1/4 cup of the batter for each fritter into the air fryer basket sprayed with cooking spray. Cook for about 6 minutes or until golden brown, then flip the fritters and cook for an additional 2 minutes.
4. In a saucepan over medium heat, melt the 1/4 cup of butter listed in the ingredients. Cook until it turns a light tan color (about 5 minutes). Remove from heat, let it cool slightly, then mix in the confectioners' sugar, remaining 1/2 teaspoon vanilla extract, and about 1-2 tablespoons of milk, adjusting for desired consistency. Drizzle this glaze over the fritters before serving.

**NUTRITIONAL SERVING**
Protein: 5g, Carbs: 58g, Fat: 12g, Sodium: 300mg, Sugar: 35g, Fiber: 2g.

**Recipe Tips:** For extra flavor, choose Honeycrisp or Granny Smith apples for their balance of sweetness and tartness which complements the cinnamon.

## 5.2 French Toast Sticks

These French Toast Sticks are a delightful twist on the classic French toast, offering a convenient and fun way to enjoy a breakfast favorite. With a hint of cinnamon and nutmeg, they provide a warm and comforting taste, perfect for a quick yet indulgent breakfast.

**PREPARATION TIME:** 10 minutes
**Cooking Time:** 6 minutes
**DIFFICULTY LEVEL:** Easy
**SERVINGS:** 2

**INGREDIENTS**
- Bread slices, 4 (preferably whole grain)
- Eggs, 2

- Ground cinnamon, 1/4 tsp
- Ground nutmeg, 1/4 tsp
- Salt, 1 pinch
- Icing sugar, 1 tsp (optional for serving)
- Butter, 2 tbsp (for cooking)

**STEPS**
1. Preheat the air fryer to 350°F (177°C)..
2. In a shallow dish, lightly beat the eggs with cinnamon, nutmeg, and a pinch of salt.
3. Slice the bread into thirds, creating stick shapes.
4. Dip each bread stick into the egg mixture, ensuring each side is well coated.
5. Cook the egg-coated bread sticks in the air fryer for 2 minutes, then flip them. If desired, brush with melted butter or spray with cooking spray for extra crispiness. Cook for another 4 minutes or until golden brown and crispy.
6. Serve hot with a sprinkle of icing sugar or a side of maple syrup.

**NUTRITIONAL SERVING**
Protein: 6g, Carbs: 20g, Fat: 10g, Sodium: 200mg, Sugar: 3g, Fiber: 1g.

**Recipe Tips:** For a lighter version, you can use a cooking spray instead of butter for cooking, and opt for whole grain bread for added health benefits.

# 5.3 Toad in the Hole Tarts (Breakfast)

This unique and delightful breakfast dish combines the flakiness of puff pastry with the richness of eggs and cheese, topped with the savory taste of ham and the freshness of chives. It's a perfect choice for a weekend brunch or a special breakfast occasion.

**PREPARATION TIME:** 5 minutes
Cooking Time: 13 minutes
**DIFFICULTY LEVEL:** Easy
**SERVINGS:** 2
**INGREDIENTS**
- Frozen puff pastry, 1 sheet
- Sliced and cooked ham, 4 tbsp
- Cheddar cheese, 4 tbsp, shredded
- Fresh chives, 1 tbsp, chopped
- Eggs, 2

**STEPS**
1. Preheat the air fryer to 400°F.

2. Lay the pastry sheet on a flat surface and cut it into 4 squares, each about 5x5 inches.
3. Place two pastry squares in the air fryer basket and cook for about 7 minutes, until they start to puff up.
4. Carefully remove the basket from the air fryer and press down the center of each pastry square to create a well. Place 1 tbsp of ham and 1 tbsp of cheddar cheese into each well.
5. Crack an egg into each well on top of the ham and cheese. Cook for an additional 6 minutes, or until the eggs are cooked to your preference.
6. Let the tarts cool for about 5 minutes after removing them from the air fryer. Repeat with the remaining pastry squares, ham, eggs, and cheese.
7. Garnish the tarts with chopped chives before serving.

**NUTRITIONAL SERVING**
Protein: 15g, Carbs: 27g, Fat: 22g, Sodium: 450mg, Sugar: 1g, Fiber: 1g.

**Recipe Tips:** For an even healthier twist, try using whole wheat puff pastry and low-fat cheese.

# 5.4 Eggs (Hard Boiled)

Hard-boiled eggs are a simple yet nutritious option, perfect for a quick breakfast, a protein-packed snack, or as an addition to salads. They are versatile, easy to prepare, and rich in essential nutrients.

**PREPARATION TIME:** 2 minutes
Cooking Time: 16 minutes
**DIFFICULTY LEVEL:** Easy
**SERVINGS:** 2

**INGREDIENTS**
- Eggs, 4

**STEPS**
1. Preheat the air fryer to 250°F.

2. Place the wire rack inside the air fryer basket and arrange the eggs on the rack.
3. Cook the eggs for about 16 minutes for a hard-boiled consistency.
4. Once cooked, immediately transfer the eggs to a bowl of ice water to stop the cooking process and cool them down.
5. Once cooled, peel the eggs and they are ready to eat or use in your recipe.

**NUTRITIONAL SERVING**

Protein: 6g, Carbs: 1g, Fat: 5g, Sodium: 62mg, Sugar: 1g, Potassium: 63mg.

**Recipe Tips:** For easier peeling, add the eggs to cold water immediately after cooking. This shrinks the egg slightly inside the shell, making it easier to remove.

## 5.5 Omelet

This classic omelet recipe is a fantastic way to start your day with a protein-rich meal. It's versatile and can be filled with a variety of vegetables and meats, making it a great option for a nutritious breakfast or a quick dinner.

**PREPARATION TIME:** 5 minutes
Cooking Time: 9 minutes
**DIFFICULTY LEVEL:** Easy
**SERVINGS:** 2

**INGREDIENTS**
- Salt, 1 pinch
- Milk, 1/4 cup
- Eggs, 2
- Shredded cheese, 1/4 cup
- Garden herbs, 1 tsp (e.g., parsley, chives)
- Vegetables and meats of choice, about 1 cup total (e.g., bell peppers, onions, cooked ham)

**STEPS**

1. In a bowl, beat the milk and eggs together until well combined.
2. Stir in the chopped vegetables and/or meats, and a pinch of salt.
3. Heat a non-stick skillet over medium heat. Pour in the egg mixture.
4. Cook for about 4-5 minutes, until the bottom is set but the top is still slightly runny.
5. Sprinkle the shredded cheese and herbs over the omelet.
6. Gently fold the omelet in half with a spatula and continue cooking for another 2-3 minutes until the cheese is melted and the omelet is cooked to your liking.
7. Carefully slide the omelet onto a plate and serve immediately.

**NUTRITIONAL SERVING**

Protein: 12g, Carbs: 2g, Fat: 15g, Sodium: 180mg, Sugar: 1g, Fiber: 0g.

**Recipe Tips:** For a fluffy omelet, whisk the eggs vigorously to incorporate air, and cook on a low to medium heat to avoid overcooking.

## 5.6 Air Fryer Egg McMuffin

This homemade version of the classic Egg McMuffin is a quick and healthier alternative to the fast-food breakfast. Made in an air fryer, it combines the goodness of eggs, cheese, and bacon, all sandwiched between a toasted muffin, making it a satisfying and portable meal.

**PREPARATION TIME:** 10 minutes
Cooking Time: 10 minutes
**DIFFICULTY LEVEL:** Easy
**SERVINGS:** 2

**INGREDIENTS**

- Eggs, 2
- Muffins, 2
- Bacon slices, 2
- Cheese slices, 2

**STEPS**

1. Preheat the Air Fryer: Set your air fryer to 400°F (approximately 204°C).
2. Prepare the Egg Cooking Setup: If you have small, air fryer-safe pans or molds, use them for cooking the eggs. Spray them with cooking oil to prevent sticking. If you don't have suitable pans, you can make makeshift containers using aluminum foil. Shape the foil into small bowls or cups that can hold an egg, and spray them with cooking oil. These foil containers should be sturdy enough to hold the egg and not collapse under its weight.
3. If using small pans or molds, place them in the air fryer and crack an egg into each. If not, create sturdy foil bowls, grease them, and then crack an egg into each. Cook in the air fryer.
4. Add the Bacon: Place the bacon slices in the air fryer basket. If space allows, they can go alongside the eggs. Otherwise, you may need to cook them in batches.
5. Cook Eggs and Bacon: Cook everything for about 5 minutes. Then, check the bacon. If it's not yet crispy, flip the slices and continue cooking for another 5 minutes. Also, check the eggs to ensure they are cooking evenly. The eggs are done when the whites are fully set and the yolks are cooked to your preference.
6. Toast the Muffins: While the eggs and bacon cook, split the muffins and toast them. You can use a traditional toaster, or if you prefer and have room, you can toast them in the air fryer once the eggs and bacon are done.
7. Assemble the Sandwiches: On one half of each toasted muffin, place a slice of cheese, then a cooked egg, followed by a slice of crispy bacon. Cap each sandwich with the other half of the muffin.

**NUTRITIONAL SERVING**

Protein: 22g, Carb: 21g, Fat: 23g, Sodium: 9g, Sugar: 11g, Potassium: 8g.

**Recipe Tips:** For a lower cholesterol option, consider using egg whites instead of whole eggs.

## 5.7 Pizza (Breakfast)

This Breakfast Pizza, made in the air fryer, is a fun and delicious way to start your day. It combines the flakiness of crescent dough with the heartiness of scrambled eggs, sausage, and cheese, topped with the fresh crunch of bell peppers.

**PREPARATION TIME:** 15 minutes

Cooking Time: 13 minutes

**DIFFICULTY LEVEL:** Hard

**SERVINGS:** 2

**INGREDIENTS**

- Crescent dough, 1 can
- Crumbled sausage, cooked, 1/2 cup
- Scrambled eggs, 3
- Minced bell pepper, 1/2
- Cheddar cheese, 1/2 cup, shredded
- Mozzarella cheese, 1/2 cup, shredded

**STEPS**

1. Preheat the air fryer to 350°F.
2. Grease a skillet or a pan that can fit into your air fryer.
3. Unroll the crescent dough and press it into the bottom of the skillet, forming a crust that covers the skillet evenly.
4. Pre-cook the crust in the air fryer for about 5 minutes or until it begins to brown.
5. Remove the skillet from the air fryer. Layer the scrambled eggs, cooked sausage, bell pepper, and both types of cheese on top of the crust.
6. Return the skillet to the air fryer and cook for an additional 8 minutes, or until the cheese is melted and bubbly.

**NUTRITIONAL SERVING**

Protein: 18g, Carbs: 25g, Fat: 22g, Sodium: 600mg, Sugar: 5g, Fiber: 1g.

**Recipe Tips:** For a healthier version, consider using turkey sausage, low-fat cheese, and whole wheat dough.

## 5.8 Cherry and Danish (Cream Cheese)

This delightful Cherry and Cream Cheese Danish is a sweet and tangy treat, perfect for a luxurious breakfast or a dessert. The combination of creamy cheese and cherry pie filling, wrapped in flaky crescent dough, creates a delightful pastry that's both comforting and indulgent.

**PREPARATION TIME:** 10 minutes
Cooking Time: 20 minutes
**DIFFICULTY LEVEL:** Easy
**SERVINGS:** 2

### INGREDIENTS

- Pillsbury Crescent Rolls Dough, 1 can
- Cream Cheese, 8 oz
- Cherry Pie Filling, 16 oz
- Icing, for serving

### STEPS

1. Preheat the air fryer to 350°F.
2. Roll out the crescent dough and separate it into individual triangles, each about 3-4 inches wide at the base.
3. Place a spoonful of cream cheese at the wider end of each dough triangle, followed by a spoonful of cherry pie filling.
4. Roll up the dough starting from the filled end, forming a crescent shape.
5. Place the prepared Danishes in the air fryer basket, ensuring they are not touching.
6. Cook the Danishes in the air fryer for 10 minutes. Then, loosely cover with foil to prevent over-browning and cook for another 7-10 minutes until golden and cooked through.
7. Remove from the air fryer and allow to cool slightly before serving with a drizzle of icing.

### NUTRITIONAL SERVING

Protein: 5g, Carbs: 40g, Fat: 18g, Sodium: 400mg, Sugar: 20g, Fiber: 1g.

**Recipe Tips:** For a lighter version, you can use reduced-fat cream cheese and a sugar-free cherry pie filling.

## 5.9 Sweet French Toast Sticks

These delightful Sweet French Toast Sticks offer a playful twist on the classic French toast. Perfect for a brunch treat or a sweet snack, they combine the comforting flavors of cinnamon and nutmeg with a crispy exterior.

**PREPARATION TIME:** 15 minutes
**Cooking Time:** 9-10 minutes
**DIFFICULTY LEVEL:** Medium
**SERVINGS:** 2

### INGREDIENTS

- 2 Large Eggs
- 4 Thick Slices of Bread
- Parchment Paper
- ¼ Cup Milk
- 1 tsp. Cinnamon
- 1 tsp. Vanilla Extract
- A Pinch of Nutmeg

### STEPS

1. Cut each slice of bread into thirds to make sticks. Line the air fryer basket with parchment paper.
2. Preheat the air fryer to 360°F.
3. In a bowl, thoroughly mix together the milk, eggs, cinnamon, vanilla extract, and nutmeg. Dip each bread stick into the egg mixture, ensuring they are well-coated. Shake off any excess.
4. Place bread sticks in the air fryer basket in a single layer, ensuring they don't touch each other. Cook in batches if necessary.

5.  Air fry the bread sticks for 4-5 minutes, then flip and continue cooking for another 5 minutes, or until they are golden and crispy.

NUTRITIONAL SERVING
Protein: 12g, Carbs: 30g, Fat: 10g, Sodium: 300mg, Sugar: 5g, Calories: ~250 kcal

**Recipe Tips:** Serve these French toast sticks with maple syrup or a fruit compote for dipping to enhance their sweetness and flavor.

# Chapter 5: Substitute Ingredients Guide

## 5.1 Apple Fritters
- **Vegan**: Substitute "Eggs" with a vegan egg replacer, "Milk" with almond or oat milk, and "Butter" with vegan butter.
- **Gluten-Free**: Replace "All-purpose flour" with "Gluten-free flour".
- **Allergen-Free**: Replace "Milk" with almond milk or oat milk, and use vegan alternatives for eggs and butter.

## 5.2 French Toast Sticks
- **Vegan**: Use vegan egg replacer, plant-based milk, and vegan butter.
- **Gluten-Free**: Replace "Bread slices" with "Gluten-free bread".
- **Allergen-Free**: Use almond milk or oat milk, and vegan egg replacer.

## 5.3 Toad in the Hole Tarts (Breakfast)
- **Vegan**: Substitute "Sliced and cooked ham" with "Vegetarian ham slices or tofu slices", "Eggs" with vegan egg replacer or tofu, and "Cheddar cheese" with vegan cheese.
- **Gluten-Free**: Use "Gluten-free puff pastry".
- **Allergen-Free**: Replace "Eggs" with a vegan egg replacer or tofu.

## 5.4 Eggs (Hard Boiled)
- **Vegan**: This recipe cannot be made vegan as it primarily consists of eggs.
- **Gluten-Free**: No substitutions needed.
- **Allergen-Free**: Eggs are a common allergen and should be avoided if allergic.

## 5.5 Omelet
- **Vegan**: Use a vegan egg replacer or tofu, and vegan cheese.
- **Gluten-Free**: No substitutions needed.
- **Allergen-Free**: Substitute "Eggs" with a vegan egg replacer or tofu.

## 5.6 Air Fryer Egg McMuffin
- **Vegan**: Replace "Eggs" with a vegan egg replacer or tofu, "Bacon slices" with vegetarian bacon or tofu slices, and "Cheese slices" with vegan cheese.
- **Gluten-Free**: Use "Gluten-free muffins".
- **Allergen-Free**: Use vegan egg replacer or tofu and vegan cheese.

## 5.7 Pizza (Breakfast)
- **Vegan**: Use vegan sausage crumbles, vegan egg replacer or tofu, and dairy-free cheese.
- **Gluten-Free**: Substitute "Crescent dough" with "Gluten-free pizza dough".
- **Allergen-Free**: Replace dairy products with vegan alternatives.

## 5.8 Cherry and Danish (Cream Cheese)
- **Vegan**: Replace "Cream Cheese" with "Dairy-free cream cheese".
- **Gluten-Free**: Use "Gluten-free crescent rolls dough".
- **Allergen-Free**: Substitute "Cream Cheese" with dairy-free cream cheese.

## 5.9 Sweet French Toast Sticks:
Vegetarian:
- No substitutions needed.

Gluten-Free:
- Thick bread: Use gluten-free bread.

Allergen-Free:
- Ensure bread and milk are allergen-free.

Please note:
- When using gluten-free flours or vegan substitutes, the texture and taste might differ slightly from the original recipe.
- The list of allergens can vary widely. Always review the ingredient list to ensure it's safe for individual dietary needs, especially for vegan and allergen-free diets.

# Chapter 6: Appetizer Recipes

## 6.1 Pickles

These fried pickles are a unique snack offering a delightful crunch with a zesty kick. The blend of dill and panko provides a crispy outer layer, while the interior remains juicy and tangy.

**PREPARATION TIME:** 15 minutes
Cooking Time: 16 minutes
**DIFFICULTY LEVEL:** Easy
**SERVINGS:** 2

**INGREDIENTS**
- Dill pickle spears, 12
- Flour, 1/2 cup
- Salt, 1/2 tsp.
- Eggs, 2
- Pickle Juice, 3 tsp.
- Garlic powder, 1/2 tsp
- Panko breadcrumbs, 1.5 cups
- Dill snipped, 2 tsp
- Cayenne, 1/2 tsp
- Cooking oil spray
- Ranch sauce (for serving)

**STEPS**
1. Preheat air fryer to 400°F. Pat dry the pickle spears and let them rest on a towel for about fifteen minutes to remove excess moisture.
2. In one bowl, mix salt and flour. In another, whisk together cayenne, garlic powder, and pickle juice. In a third bowl, mix dill and panko breadcrumbs.
3. Coat the pickle spears first in the flour mixture, then dip into the pickle juice mixture, and finally press into the dill and panko mixture.
4. Arrange the pickles in the air fryer basket in a single layer and spray with cooking oil. Air fry for 8 minutes, flip, then spray again and continue cooking for another 8 minutes until golden and crispy.
5. Serve hot with ranch sauce, if desired.

**NUTRITIONAL SERVING**
Protein: 3g, Carbohydrates: 16g, Fat: 1g, Sodium: 2g, Sugar: 2g.

**Recipe Tips:** For an extra flavor boost, try adding smoked paprika to the panko breadcrumb mixture. It adds a subtle smokiness that complements the tanginess of the pickles.

## 6.2 Zesty Tofu Sriracha Spring Rolls - A Crunchy Delight

Enjoy the vibrant fusion of spicy Sriracha and crispy tofu in these delightful spring rolls. The fresh vegetables add a crunch, while the tofu provides a satisfying protein punch, making it a perfect appetizer or light meal.

**PREPARATION TIME:** 20 minutes
Cooking Time: 10 minutes
**DIFFICULTY LEVEL:** Easy
**SERVINGS:** 4

**INGREDIENTS**
- Extra Firm Tofu, 1 block (14 oz, drained and cut into thin strips)
- Sriracha Sauce, 4 tablespoons
- Brown Rice Paper, 8 pieces
- Fresh Spring Mix, 4 cups
- Shredded Carrots, 1 cup
- Red Bell Pepper, 1 (thinly sliced)

- Cilantro, a handful (roughly chopped)
- Chives, a handful (roughly chopped)
- Low-sodium Soy Sauce, 2 tablespoons
- Sesame Oil, 1 tablespoon
- Avocado, 1 (sliced)
- Lime, 1 (cut into wedges for serving)
- Water (for soaking rice paper)

## STEPS

1. Begin by preheating your Air Fryer to 375°F (190°C). Toss the tofu strips in the soy sauce and sesame oil, then air fry them for about 10 minutes, flipping halfway through, until golden and crispy.
2. Prepare the Sriracha Sauce: Combine Sriracha with the juice of half a lime. Adjust to taste - you may add more lime juice for a tangier finish.
3. Soak the brown rice paper in water until soft. On a clean work surface, lay a sheet flat. Add a handful of spring mix, shredded carrots, sliced bell pepper, tofu strips, avocado slices, cilantro, and chives. Drizzle with Sriracha sauce.
4. Fold the edges of the rice paper over the filling, then roll it up tightly, like a burrito. Repeat until all ingredients are used.
5. Cut each roll in half diagonally and serve with lime wedges and extra Sriracha sauce for dipping.

## NUTRITIONAL SERVING

Protein: 12g, Ca Protein: 12g, Carbohydrates: 25g, Fat: 7g, Sodium: 300mg, Sugar: 3g, Fiber: 3.

**Recipe Tips:** To add more texture, consider including thinly sliced cucumber or mango for a sweet and crunchy contrast.

## 6.3 Fiesta Chicken Fingers

Fiesta Chicken Fingers offer a delightful blend of crispy texture and spicy flavors, making them a perfect snack or party appetizer. This recipe combines the zesty taste of taco seasoning with the crunch of corn chips for a fun twist on the classic chicken fingers.

**PREPARATION TIME:** 20 minutes
Cooking Time: 16 minutes
**DIFFICULTY LEVEL:** Easy
**SERVINGS:** 2

## INGREDIENTS

- Boneless and skinless chicken breasts, ¾ pound
- Buttermilk, ½ cup
- Pepper, ¼ tsp.
- Flour, 1 cup
- Crushed maize chips, 2 cups
- Taco seasoning, 1 envelope (approx. 1 oz)
- Vegetable oil (for spraying)
- Sour cream ranch (for serving, quantity to taste)

## STEPS

1. Preheat the air fryer to 402°F. Use a meat mallet to pound chicken breasts to an even thickness.
2. In a bowl, mix pepper and buttermilk. In another bowl, add flour. In a third bowl, combine taco seasoning and crushed maize chips.
3. Dip chicken first in flour, ensuring each piece is coated, then dip in buttermilk mixture, and finally in maize chip mixture, pressing to adhere.
4. Spray chicken with vegetable oil and place in the air fryer basket. Cook for 8 minutes on each side until golden brown and fully cooked.
5. Serve with sour cream ranch dip.

## NUTRITIONAL SERVING

Protein: 24g, Carb: 60g, Fat: 36g, Sodium: 22g, Sugar: 23g, Potassium: 13g.

**Recipe Tips:** For an extra kick, mix some chili powder or cayenne pepper into the flour for a spicier coating.

## 6.4 Cheeseburger Onion Rings

Cheeseburger Onion Rings are a unique and delicious fusion of two classic favorites. These rings feature a juicy, savory filling of ground beef and cheese, coated in a crispy breadcrumb crust. They are perfect for a fun appetizer or a playful side dish.

**PREPARATION TIME:** 25 minutes
Cooking Time: 14 minutes
**DIFFICULTY LEVEL:** Easy
**SERVINGS:** 2

**INGREDIENTS**
- Lean ground beef, 1 pound
- Ketchup, ⅓ cup
- Mustard, 2 tsp.
- Salt, ½ tsp.
- Onion, 1 (large)
- Cheddar cheese, 4 ounces, sliced or shredded
- Flour, ¾ cup
- Garlic powder, 2 tbsp.
- Eggs, 2
- Panko breadcrumbs, 1½ cups
- Cooking spray
- 

**STEPS**
1. Preheat the air fryer to 335°F. In a bowl, combine ground beef, ketchup, mustard, and salt.
2. Cut the onion into half-inch thick rings. Stuff each ring with the beef mixture and a piece of cheddar cheese.
3. In a bowl, mix flour and garlic powder. In separate bowls, place beaten eggs and breadcrumbs.
4. Coat each onion ring in flour, dip in egg, then press into breadcrumbs.

5. Arrange rings in the air fryer basket in a single layer. Spray with cooking oil. Air fry for 14 minutes, flipping halfway through, until golden brown and the beef is fully cooked.

**NUTRITIONAL SERVING**
Protein: 19g, Carb: 19g, Fat: 11g, Sodium: 12g, Sugar: 10g, Potassium: 14g.

**Recipe Tips:** For extra flavor, mix a pinch of cayenne pepper into the flour mixture.

## 6.5 Garlic Rosemary Sprouts

Garlic Rosemary Sprouts offer a delightful combination of aromatic rosemary and pungent garlic, bringing out the natural flavors of Brussels sprouts. This dish is perfect for those seeking a healthy yet flavorful side.

**PREPARATION TIME:** 20 minutes
**Cooking Time**: 13 minutes
**DIFFICULTY LEVEL:** Medium
**SERVINGS:** 2

**INGREDIENTS**
- Olive oil, 1 tbsp.
- Minced garlic, 2 cloves
- Salt, ½ tsp.
- Pepper, ¼ tsp.
- Brussels sprouts, 1 pound, halved and trimmed
- Panko breadcrumbs, ½ cup
- Chopped rosemary, 1 tsp.

**STEPS**
1. Preheat the air fryer to 352°F. In a small bowl, heat olive oil with minced garlic, salt, and pepper in the microwave for about 30 seconds.
2. Toss the Brussels sprouts in the garlic oil mixture. Arrange them in the air-fryer basket and cook for 5 minutes. Shake the basket, then continue air frying for another 8 minutes until sprouts are tender and lightly browned.

3. Toss breadcrumbs with the remaining oil mixture and chopped rosemary. Sprinkle over the cooked sprouts and air fry for an additional 5 minutes until the breadcrumbs are golden brown.

**NUTRITIONAL SERVING**
Protein: 5g, Carb: 15g, Fat: 11g, Sodium: 9g, Sugar: 12g, Potassium: 10g.

**Recipe Tips:** Try roasting the garlic before mixing with olive oil for a milder, sweeter flavor.

## 6.6 Taquitos

These tantalizing Taquitos, cooked to perfection in an air fryer, offer a delightful crunch encasing a spicy beef filling. They're a perfect snack for those craving a bite of Mexican-inspired goodness.

**PREPARATION TIME:** 15 minutes
Cooking Time: 13 minutes
**DIFFICULTY LEVEL:** Hard
**SERVINGS:** 6

**INGREDIENTS**
- Eggs, 2
- Dry breadcrumbs, ½ cup
- Taco seasoning, ½ tsp.
- Lean ground beef, 1 pound
- Corn tortillas, 6
- Salsa and Guacamole (for serving)
- Cooking spray

**STEPS**
1. Preheat air fryer to 352 °F. Combine the breadcrumbs, taco spice and eggs in a bowl. Add the beef and mix gently but well.

2. Lay a quarter cup of the beef mixture down the middle of each tortilla. Roll up the tortilla tightly around the filling and secure it with toothpicks. Place the taquitos in a single layer on the oiled tray in the air-fryer basket. Spray with cooking oil. Air fry for about six minutes, then flip and continue air frying until the meat is fully cooked and the taquitos are golden brown and crispy, about seven more minutes. Remove the toothpicks and serve with guacamole and salsa, if desired.

**NUTRITIONAL SERVING**
Protein: 10g, Carb: 12g, Fat: 9g, Sodium: 8g, Sugar: 7g, Potassium: 8g.

**Recipe Tips:** For an even crisp, do not overcrowd the air fryer basket and ensure each taquito is evenly spaced.

## 6.7 Mozzarella Sticks

Enjoy a crispy, cheesy delight with these air-fried Mozzarella Sticks. Perfect as a snack or side dish, they offer a guilt-free way to indulge in your favorite comfort food.

**PREPARATION TIME:** 15 minutes
**Cooking Time:** 15-16 minutes
**DIFFICULTY LEVEL:** Easy
**SERVINGS:** 2

**INGREDIENTS**
- For Batter:
- Water, 1/2 cup
- Flour, 1/4 cup
- Cornstarch, 5 tsp
- Cornmeal, 1 tbsp
- Garlic powder, 1 tsp
- Salt, 1/2 tsp
- For Coatings:
- Breadcrumbs, 1 cup

- Salt, 1/2 tsp
- Black pepper, 1/2 tsp
- Dried parsley flakes, 1/2 tsp
- Garlic powder, 1/2 tsp
- Onion powder, 1/4 tsp
- Dried oregano, 1/4 tsp
- Dried basil, 1/4 tsp

Mozzarella cheese, 5 ounces
Flour, for dusting
Cooking spray

## STEPS

1. In a bowl, whisk together water, flour, cornstarch, cornmeal, garlic powder, and salt for the batter. Adjust consistency as needed.
2. In another bowl, mix breadcrumbs, salt, pepper, parsley, garlic powder, onion powder, oregano, and basil for the coating.
3. Dust each mozzarella stick with flour. Dip in batter, then roll in breadcrumb mixture. Arrange on a baking sheet and freeze for at least 1 hour.
4. Preheat air fryer to 450°F. Place mozzarella sticks in the basket, spray lightly with cooking spray. Cook for 6 minutes, flip, and continue cooking for another 9-10 minutes until lightly browned.

## NUTRITIONAL SERVING

Protein: 2.8g, Carbs: 18g, Fat: 0g, Sodium: 1g, Sugar: 2g, Potassium: 2g, Calories: Approx. 150 kcal.

**Recipe Tips:** For extra crispiness, double coat the mozzarella sticks with batter and breadcrumbs.

## 6.8 Balsamic Glazed Chicken Wings

Savor the rich and tangy taste of Balsamic Glazed Chicken Wings, where the succulence of the chicken is perfectly complemented by the balsamic reduction. A delightful blend of sweet and savory that's hard to resist!

**PREPARATION TIME:** 10 minutes
**Cooking Time:** 25 minutes
**DIFFICULTY LEVEL:** Easy
**SERVINGS:** 2

## INGREDIENTS

For coatings
- Cooking spray
- Baking powder, 3 tbsp
- Salt, 2 tbsp
- Freshly ground black pepper, 1 tbsp
- Paprika, 1 tsp
- Chicken wings, 2 pounds

For the glaze
- Water, 1/3 cup
- Balsamic vinegar, 1/3 cup
- Soy sauce, 2 tsp
- Honey, 2 tsp
- Chili sauce, 2 tsp
- Garlic cloves, minced, 2
- Cornstarch, 1 tsp

For the garnish
- Green onion, chopped, 1
- Sesame seeds, 1/4 tsp

## STEPS

1. Preheat air fryer to 385°F and coat the basket with cooking spray.
2. Mix baking powder, pepper, paprika, and salt in a bowl. Toss chicken wings in the mixture to coat evenly. Shake off excess.
3. Place wings in the air fryer basket, ensuring they're not overcrowded. Air fry for 20 minutes, shaking halfway through. Increase the temperature to 450°F and air fry for an additional 5 minutes to crisp up.

4. Meanwhile, in a saucepan, combine balsamic vinegar, honey, soy sauce, chili sauce, water, and minced garlic. Bring to a boil and reduce to a simmer for about 15 minutes. Mix cornstarch with a teaspoon of water and add to the sauce to thicken.

5. Toss the crispy wings in the glaze and garnish with sesame seeds and green onion.

**NUTRITIONAL SERVING**
Protein: 32g, Carbs: 32g, Fat: 22g, Sodium: 2g, Sugar: 2g, Potassium: 3g, Calories: Approx. 400 kcal.

**Recipe Tips:** To ensure even cooking, don't overcrowd the wings in the air fryer. Cook in batches if necessary.

## 6.9 Arancini

Arancini, classic Italian rice balls, combine the creaminess of risotto with a crunchy exterior. These air-fried delights are perfect as appetizers or snacks.

**PREPARATION TIME:** 20 minutes
**Cooking Time:** 9 minutes
**DIFFICULTY LEVEL:** Easy
**SERVINGS:** 2

**INGREDIENTS**
- Chicken, 3 large
- Cooked rice, 1/2 cup
- Grated Parmesan cheese, 2/3 cup
- Melted butter, 1/3 cup
- Italian seasoning, 1/2 tsp.
- Salt, 1/2 tsp.
- Black pepper, 1/4 tsp.
- Mozzarella cheese, 2 ounces, cubed
- Breadcrumbs, 1 cup
- Cooking spray

**STEPS**

1. In a large bowl, lightly beat two eggs. Add Parmesan cheese, Italian seasoning, butter, 1/4 tsp. salt, and 1/2 tsp. pepper. Mix well and chill for 20 minutes.

2. Preheat air fryer to 375°F (190°C).

3. Form the rice mixture into 1 1/2-inch balls, inserting a cube of mozzarella in the center of each.

4. Coat each ball in breadcrumbs and place in the air fryer basket, sprayed with cooking spray.

5. Air fry for 6 minutes, then increase heat to 450°F and cook for an additional 3 minutes for a crispy exterior.

**NUTRITIONAL SERVING**
Protein: 15g, Carbs: 21g, Fat: 38g, Sodium: 200mg, Sugar: 2g, Potassium: 300mg, Calories: ~450 kcal.

**Recipe Tips:** Chill the rice mixture thoroughly before shaping to prevent the arancini from falling apart during cooking.

## 6.10 Mac and Cheese Ball

Indulge in the ultimate comfort food with these Mac and Cheese Balls. Crispy on the outside, creamy and cheesy on the inside, these balls are a delightful twist on the classic mac and cheese.

**PREPARATION TIME:** 20 minutes
**Cooking Time:** 12-16 minutes
**DIFFICULTY LEVEL:** Hard
**SERVINGS:** 2

**INGREDIENTS**
- Water, 6 cups
- Macaroni and cheese, 7.12-ounce package
- Milk, 1/4 cup
- Margarine, 4 tbsp
- Sharp cheddar cheese, shredded, 3/4 cup
- Nonstick cooking spray

- Panko breadcrumbs, 1/2 cup
- Regular breadcrumbs, 1/2 cup
- Salt, 1/2 tsp
- Garlic powder, 1/2 tbsp
- Eggs, 2, beaten

**STEPS**

1. Boil water in a large pot. Add macaroni from the package and cook for 6 to 8 minutes, stirring occasionally, until tender. Drain and return to the pot.
2. Stir in milk and margarine to create the cheese sauce. Add the cheddar cheese and stir until evenly melted and mixed.
3. Chill the macaroni and cheese until firm, between 2 hours to overnight.
4. Shape the mixture into 1/2-inch balls and arrange on a parchment-lined baking sheet.
5. Preheat the air fryer to 355°F. Spray the basket with nonstick cooking spray.
6. In a medium bowl, mix panko, breadcrumbs, salt, and garlic powder. Dip each ball first in the beaten eggs, then in the panko mixture.
7. Place the balls in the air fryer basket, ensuring they are in a single layer and not touching. Cook in batches if necessary.
8. Air fry for 8 to 12 minutes, then flip and cook for an additional 3 to 4 minutes or until lightly browned.

**NUTRITIONAL SERVING**

Protein: 3g, Carbs: 9g, Fat: 4g, Sodium: 200mg, Sugar: 2g, Potassium: 300mg, Calories: Approx. 150-200 kcal per serving.

**Recipe Tips:** For extra flavor, mix some herbs or spices like paprika or dried basil into the breadcrumb coating.

## 6.11 Taco

Indulge in the savory and delicious flavors of homemade tacos. These are perfect for a quick and flavorful meal, combining the classic taste of seasoned ground sirloin with the fresh textures of beans, corn, and tomatoes, wrapped in a crisp corn tortilla.

**PREPARATION TIME:** 10 minutes
**Cooking Time:** 20 minutes
**DIFFICULTY LEVEL:** Easy
**SERVINGS:** 2

**INGREDIENTS**
- 4-inch Corn Tortillas
- Oil for frying
- Sea Salt, to taste
- 1 Small Onion, chopped
- 2 Garlic Cloves, minced
- 1 1/2 lbs. Ground Sirloin
- 1 Taco Seasoning Packet
- 1 15 oz can Pinto Beans
- 1 15 oz can Corn
- 1 15 oz can Diced Tomatoes
- 1 cup Salsa
- Chicken (optional)
- Sliced Cheddar Cheese and Sour Cream for topping

**STEPS**

1. Heat a large nonstick skillet with 1/6 to 1/4 inches of oil over medium heat until simmering. Gently heat tortillas in the air fryer, cooking them until they bubble and start to slightly brown, then flip and cook for an additional couple of minutes. Sprinkle with sea salt. Continue with remaining tortillas.
2. In a soup pot, heat over medium-high heat with a tablespoon of oil. Sauté onion and garlic for about 2 minutes until fragrant.
3. Add taco seasoning and cook for about a minute.
4. Incorporate beans, corn, broth, tomatoes, and salsa. Bring to a simmer, stirring frequently.
5. Reduce heat to low, cover the pot, and let simmer gently for at least 20 minutes.
6. Serve the soup with freshly prepared tortillas, topped with fried chicken, grated cheese, and sour cream.

**NUTRITIONAL SERVING**

Protein: 15g, Carbs: 100g, Fat: 13g, Sodium: 200mg, Sugar: 2g, Calories: ~800 kcal

**Recipe Tips:** For an even healthier option, use lean ground turkey instead of sirloin, and add more vegetables like bell peppers or zucchini to the mix.

# Chapter 6: Substitute Ingredients Guide

## 6.1 Pickles
- Vegan:
    - Eggs -> Chickpea flour (mix with water to create a batter)
- Gluten-Free:
    - Flour -> Gluten-free flour
    - Panko breadcrumbs -> Gluten-free breadcrumbs
- Allergen-Free:
    - Eggs -> Chickpea flour (mix with water to create a batter)

## 6.2 Zesty Tofu Sriracha Spring Rolls - A Crunchy Delight
- Vegan:
    - Recipe is already vegan.
- Gluten-Free:
    - Brown Rice Paper -> Ensure it's gluten-free (most are, but double-check)
    - Low-sodium Soy Sauce -> Tamari or gluten-free soy sauce
- Allergen-Free:
    - Soy Sauce -> Coconut aminos
    - Sesame Oil -> Olive oil

## 6.3 Fiesta Chicken Fingers
- Vegan:
    - Boneless and skinless chicken breasts -> Firm tofu or tempeh slices
- Gluten-Free:
    - Flour -> Gluten-free flour
- Allergen-Free:
    - Buttermilk -> Plant-based milk (like almond or oat) with a tsp of lemon juice

## 6.4 Cheeseburger Onion Rings
- Vegan:
    - Lean ground beef -> Vegan ground meat substitute (like textured vegetable protein or store-bought vegan ground meat)
    - Cheddar cheese -> Vegan cheese
    - Eggs -> Chickpea flour (mix with water to create a batter)
- Gluten-Free:

- Flour -> Gluten-free flour
- Panko crumbs -> Gluten-free breadcrumbs

## 6.5 Garlic Rosemary Sprouts
- Vegan:
    - Recipe is already vegan.
- Gluten-Free:
    - Panko breadcrumbs -> Gluten-free breadcrumbs

## 6.6 Taquitos
- Vegan:
    - Lean ground beef -> Vegan ground meat substitute (like lentils or store-bought vegan ground meat)
- Gluten-Free:
    - Tortillas corn -> Ensure they're gluten-free (most are, but double-check)
- Allergen-Free:
    - Eggs -> Chickpea flour (mix with water to create a batter)
    -

## 6.7 Mozzarella Sticks:
- **Vegetarian**: No substitutions needed. All ingredients are vegetarian.
- **Gluten-Free:**
    - Flour: Use gluten-free all-purpose flour.
    - Cornmeal: Ensure it's gluten-free or substitute with gluten-free breadcrumbs.
    - Breadcrumbs: Use gluten-free breadcrumbs.
- **Allergen-Free:** Mozzarella cheese: Use dairy-free mozzarella.

## 6.8 Balsamic Glazed Chicken Wings:
Vegetarian:
- Chicken legs: Substitute with cauliflower wings or tofu pieces. **Gluten-Free:**
- Soy sauce: Use gluten-free tamari. **Allergen-Free:**
- Soy sauce: Use coconut aminos as a substitute.

## 6.9 Arancini:
Vegetarian:

- Chickens: This seems like an error in the recipe. If chicken is an ingredient, replace with mushrooms or vegetable of choice. **Gluten-Free:**
- Breadcrumbs: Use gluten-free breadcrumbs. **Allergen-Free:**
- Parmesan cheese & Mozzarella cheese: Use dairy-free versions.

## 6.10 Mac and Cheese Ball:
Vegetarian:
- Ensure the macaroni and cheese mix doesn't have non-vegetarian ingredients. **Gluten-Free:**
- Macaroni: Use gluten-free macaroni.
- Breadcrumbs & Panko breadcrumbs: Use gluten-free breadcrumbs. **Allergen-Free:**
- Milk: Use dairy-free milk like almond or soy.
- Margarine: Ensure it's dairy-free or use coconut oil.
- Cheddar cheese: Use dairy-free cheddar.

## 6.11 Taco
Vegetarian:
- Ground sirloin: Replace with a plant-based ground meat substitute available at most grocery stores, or consider using extra beans, lentils, or mushrooms as a meaty filler.
- Chicken: Omit or use a plant-based chicken substitute.

Gluten-Free:
- Corn tortillas: Ensure they are labeled gluten-free as some brands may contain traces of wheat.

- Taco seasoning: Some taco seasonings can contain wheat as a filler or thickening agent. Ensure you use a gluten-free variety or make your own using individual spices.

Allergen-Free:
- Corn tortillas: Some might contain additives or preservatives. Opt for pure, all-natural corn tortillas without added allergens.
- Sliced cheddar cheese: Omit or use a dairy-free cheese substitute.
- Sour cream: Omit or use a dairy-free sour cream substitute.
- Taco seasoning: As mentioned, some may contain wheat or other allergens. Always read labels or prepare your own seasoning mix.

6.8 General Tso's Cauliflower
- Vegan:
  - Recipe is already vegan.
- Gluten-Free:
  - Flour -> Gluten-free flour
  - Soy sauce -> Tamari or gluten-free soy sauce
- Allergen-Free:
  - Soy Sauce -> Coconut aminos
  - Sesame Oil -> Olive oil

**Note:** Always check the labels of store-bought ingredients for hidden allergens, especially when catering for vegans and individuals with severe allergies. Ensure that all products are produced in a vegan and allergen-free environment, as needed.

# Chapter 7: First Course Recipes

## 7.1 Bang Chicken

Bang Chicken is a delightful mix of sweet and spicy flavors, perfectly coating tender chicken. Ideal for those who appreciate the harmony of honey's sweetness with Sriracha's heat.

**PREPARATION TIME:** 15 minutes
Cooking Time: 18 minutes
**DIFFICULTY LEVEL:** Medium
**SERVINGS:** 2

**INGREDIENTS**
- Mayonnaise, 1/2 cup
- Honey, 2 tbsp.
- Sriracha sauce, 1/2 tbsp.
- Chicken, 1/2 kg
- Buttermilk, 1 cup
- Flour, ¾ cup
- Cornstarch, ½ cup
- Egg, 1
- Breadcrumbs (quantity as needed for coating)
- Oil (quantity as needed for frying)

**STEPS**
1. To create the Bang Chicken sauce, blend mayonnaise, honey, and Sriracha sauce in a food processor until smooth.
2. In a separate mixing bowl, combine the egg, flour, cornstarch, buttermilk, a pinch of salt, and pepper. Whisk until fully combined to prepare the batter.
3. Coat the chicken pieces in the buttermilk batter and then in breadcrumbs. Place them in the air fryer in batches. Air fry at 375°F for about 9 minutes or until the chicken is fully cooked, flipping the chicken pieces halfway through.
4. Serve the Bang Chicken with a side of your choice, such as eggs or leafy greens.

**NUTRITIONAL SERVING**
Protein: 21g, Carbohydrates: 23g, Fat: 10g, Sodium: 12mg, Sugar: 10g, Potassium: 13mg..

**Recipe Tips:** To ensure a crispier texture, thoroughly coat the chicken with the batter and breadcrumbs before air frying.

## 7.2 Crispy Air Fryer Eggplant Parmesan

This recipe offers a healthier twist to the classic Eggplant Parmesan. Crispy on the outside and tender on the inside, these air fryer slices are topped with tangy marinara and melty mozzarella.

**PREPARATION TIME:** 10 minutes
Cooking Time: 10 minutes
**DIFFICULTY LEVEL:** Medium
**SERVINGS:** 2

**INGREDIENTS**
- Eggplant, 1
- Wheat breadcrumbs, ½ cup
- Parmesan cheese, 3 tbsp.
- Italian seasoning, 1 tsp.
- Salt
- Flour, 3 tbsp.
- Water, 1 tbsp.
- Olive oil spray
- Marinara sauce, 1 cup
- Mozzarella cheese, ¼ cup
- Egg, 1
- Parsley

**STEPS**
1. Slice the eggplant into half-inch-thick rounds. Sprinkle salt on both sides of each slice and set aside for about 10 minutes to draw out moisture..

2. In a bowl, create a batter by whisking together the egg, water, and flour.
3. In another shallow bowl, mix together the wheat breadcrumbs, Parmesan cheese, Italian seasoning, and a pinch of salt.
4. Dip each eggplant slice in the batter, ensuring even coverage. Then coat it with the breadcrumb mixture.
5. Place the coated eggplant slices on a plate. Spray lightly with olive oil.
6. Preheat the air fryer to 360°F. Place the eggplant slices in the basket in a single layer and air fry for about 8 minutes.
7. Top each slice with a spoonful of marinara sauce and a sprinkle of mozzarella cheese. Return to the air fryer and cook until the cheese is melted and bubbly, about 2 more minutes.
8. Serve the eggplant Parmesan with a sprinkle of chopped parsley and optionally, alongside spaghetti.

### Nutritional Serving

Protein: 8g, Carbohydrates: 45g, Fat: 22g, Sodium: 320mg, Sugar: 25g, Potassium: 340mg.

## 7.3 Roasted Brussels Sprouts With Balsamic

Experience the rich flavors of Brussels sprouts enhanced with the tangy taste of balsamic vinegar. A simple yet delightful dish that brings out the natural sweetness of the sprouts with a hint of acidity, making it a perfect side for any meal.

**Preparation time:** 15 minutes
Cooking Time: 18 minutes
**Difficulty Level:** Easy
**Servings:** 2

### Ingredients
- Brussels sprouts, 1 pound (halved)
- Olive oil, 2 tbsp.
- Balsamic vinegar, 1 tbsp.
- Black Pepper, to taste
- Salt , to taste

### Steps
1. Toss the halved Brussels sprouts in a bowl with olive oil and balsamic vinegar.
2. Season with salt and pepper, and toss again to ensure even coating.
3. Place the seasoned sprouts in the air fryer basket.
4. Air fry at 359°F for 18 minutes, shaking the basket halfway through the cooking time for even browning and cooking.
5. Serve hot, seasoned with additional salt and pepper if desired.

### Nutritional Serving

Protein: 5g, Carbs: 15g, Fat: 11g, Sodium: 9mg, Sugar: 5g, Potassium: 13g.

**Recipe Tips:** For an extra touch of flavor, roast a garlic clove with the sprouts, or sprinkle with a bit of grated Parmesan cheese before serving.

## 7.4 Chicken Nuggets

Delight in these crispy, homemade air fryer chicken nuggets. Perfectly seasoned and coated for a golden crunch, they are a healthier alternative to the traditional fried version, yet just as satisfying.

**Preparation time:** 20 minutes
Cooking Time: 12 minutes
**Difficulty Level:** Hard
**Servings:** 2

## INGREDIENTS

- Chicken breasts, 2 (cut into nugget-sized pieces)
- Buttermilk, to soak
- Flour, for coating
- Eggs, beaten, for dipping
- Panko breadcrumbs, 1.5 cups
- Parmesan cheese, ¼ cup
- Sweet paprika, 2 tsp.
- Cooking spray

## STEPS

1. Soak the chicken pieces in buttermilk while preparing the coatings.
2. In a bowl, mix flour, Parmesan cheese, paprika, and a pinch of salt.
3. Dip each chicken piece in the flour mixture, then into the beaten eggs, and finally coat with panko breadcrumbs.
4. Preheat the air fryer to 400°F. Spray the basket with cooking spray.
5. Place the chicken nuggets in the basket in a single layer, ensuring they do not touch. Spray the tops with cooking spray.
6. Air fry for 10 minutes, then flip the nuggets and continue air frying for an additional 2 minutes or until golden brown and cooked through.

## NUTRITIONAL SERVING

Protein: 85g, Carb: 25g, Fat: 14g, Sodium: 21g, Sugar: 17g, Potassium: 15g.

**Recipe Tips:** For an extra flavor boost, add a pinch of garlic powder or onion powder to the breadcrumb mixture.

## 7.5 Dumplings

Enjoy a delightful taste of Asian cuisine with these air fryer dumplings. Crispy on the outside and juicy inside, they make a perfect appetizer or snack.

**PREPARATION TIME:** 20 minutes
Cooking Time: 10 minutes

**DIFFICULTY LEVEL:** Medium
**SERVINGS:** 2

## INGREDIENTS

- Chicken dumplings, 8 ounces (frozen)
- Soy sauce, 1/4 cup
- Water, 1/4 cup
- Maple syrup, 1/8 cup
- Garlic powder, 1/2 tsp.
- Rice vinegar, 1/2 tsp.
- Red pepper flakes, a pinch
- Cooking spray

## STEPS

1. Preheat the air fryer to 370°F.
2. Lightly spray the frozen dumplings with cooking spray and arrange them in a single layer in the air fryer basket.
3. Air fry for about 5 minutes, then turn the dumplings and lightly spray again.
4. Continue air frying for another 5 minutes or until the dumplings are golden brown and crispy.
5. In the meantime, mix soy sauce, water, maple syrup, garlic powder, rice vinegar, and red pepper flakes in a bowl to prepare the dipping sauce.
6. Serve the crispy dumplings with the dipping sauce.

## NUTRITIONAL SERVING

Protein: 21g, Carb: 23g, Fat: 10g, Sodium: 6g, Sugar: 8g, Potassium: 5g.

**Recipe Tips:** For an extra crispy texture, ensure the dumplings are not touching each other in the air fryer.

## 7.6 Pork Special Chops

Savor the rich flavors of these Pork Special Chops, perfectly seasoned and air fried to juicy perfection. A delightful main course that pairs well with various side dishes.

**PREPARATION TIME:** 20 minutes

Cooking Time: 14 minutes

**DIFFICULTY LEVEL:** Hard

**SERVINGS:** 2

**INGREDIENTS**

- Boneless pork chops, 4
- Grill seasoning, 1 tbsp.
- Maple syrup, 1/4 cup
- Dijon mustard, 2 tbsp.
- Lemon juice, 2 tsp.
- Vegetable oil
- Salt, 1/2 tsp.

**STEPS**

1. Lightly oil the air-fryer basket.
2. Pat the pork chops dry with paper towels and season each side with grill seasoning.
3. Arrange the pork chops in a single layer in the air fryer basket. Depending on the size of your air fryer, you might need to cook in batches.
4. Air fry at 375°F for about 14 minutes, flipping the pork chops halfway through the cooking time.
5. The pork chops are ready when their internal temperature reaches 145°F.
6. While the pork chops are cooking, mix lemon juice, salt, and maple syrup in a separate bowl.
7. Immediately after removing the pork chops from the air fryer, apply the sauce.
8. Let the pork chops rest for 2 minutes before serving.

**NUTRITIONAL SERVING**

Protein: 20g, Carb: 11g, Fat: 1g, Sodium: 2g, Sugar: 5g, Potassium: 4g.

**Recipe Tips:** For even cooking, ensure that the pork chops are of uniform thickness before air frying.

## 7.7 Chicken Chimichangas

Delight in the tantalizing flavors of Chicken Chimichangas, a perfect blend of tender chicken, zesty salsa, and rice, all wrapped in a crispy tortilla. A true treat for any Mexican cuisine lover.

**PREPARATION TIME:** 25 minutes

Cooking Time: 8 minutes

**DIFFICULTY LEVEL:** Medium

**SERVINGS:** 2

**INGREDIENTS**

- Rotisserie chicken, shredded, 1 cup
- Cooked rice, 1 1/2 cups
- Salsa, 1 cup
- Salt, 1/2 tsp.
- Flour tortillas (Soft taco), 8 inches, 4
- Vegetable oil, 2 tbsp.

**STEPS**

1. Lightly oil the bottom of the air fryer basket and preheat to 360°F.
2. Mix the shredded chicken, rice, salsa, and salt in a bowl.
3. Place approximately half a cup of the chicken mixture in the center of each tortilla. Tightly fold the sides over the filling.
4. Place the chimichangas in the oiled basket, seam side down. Lightly brush the tops with vegetable oil.
5. Air-fry for 4 minutes, then use tongs to flip the chimichangas. Continue air-frying until they turn golden and crispy, about 4 more minutes.
6. Optional: Store the filling in an airtight container in the refrigerator for up to two days if not used immediately.
7. Serve the chimichangas topped with guacamole, diced onion, shredded spinach, garlic sour cream sauce, and white cheese sauce, if desired.

Protein: 125g, Carbs: 95g, Fat: 25g, Sodium: 1200mg, Sugar: 18g, Potassium: 800mg.

**Recipe Tips:** For a healthier version, use whole wheat tortillas and add more vegetables like bell peppers or corn to the filling.

## 7.8 Simple Chicken Burrito Bowls

Experience the fusion of flavors in these Simple Chicken Burrito Bowls, featuring a hearty mix of rotisserie chicken, black beans, and corn, all served over fluffy rice. It's a quick, nutritious, and satisfying meal.

**PREPARATION TIME:** 10 minutes
**Cooking Time**: 18 minutes
**DIFFICULTY LEVEL:** Easy
**SERVINGS:** 2

### INGREDIENTS
- Rotisserie chicken, shredded, 1 cup
- Black beans, 1 15 oz can, drained and rinsed
- Corn, 1 15 oz can, drained
- Taco skillet sauce, 1 8 oz packet
- Vegetable oil, 1 tbsp.
- White rice, 1 cup
- Salt, 1 tsp.
- Water, 1 3/4 cups
- Taco sauce, 2 tbsp.
- Iceberg lettuce, 1 cup, shredded
- Avocado, 1, diced
- Lime wedges, for serving
- Cheddar cheese, shredded, 6 oz
- Sour cream, for serving
- Jalapenos, sliced, 4 oz

### STEPS

1. In a saucepan, combine the shredded chicken, black beans, corn, and taco skillet sauce. Cook over medium heat, stirring occasionally, until heated through and simmering.
2. In a separate saucepan, heat the oil over medium heat. Add the rice, water, salt, and taco sauce. Bring to a boil, then reduce heat, cover, and simmer for 18 minutes until the liquid is absorbed and the rice is tender.
3. Assemble the burrito bowls: Scoop rice into bowls, then top with the chicken, bean, and corn mixture.
4. Garnish with shredded lettuce, diced avocado, shredded cheddar cheese, sour cream, jalapenos, and lime wedges.

### NUTRITIONAL SERVING

Protein: 95g, Carbs: 40g, Fat: 22g, Sodium: 1400mg, Sugar: 17g, Potassium: 600mg.

**Recipe Tips:** Add a splash of lime juice to the rice while cooking for a zesty flavor.

## 7.9 Chicken Soft Tacos

Savor the rich flavors of Chicken Soft Tacos, a delightful combination of juicy chicken, zesty orange and chipotle, wrapped in soft tortillas. Perfect for a quick and satisfying meal.

**PREPARATION TIME:** 15 minutes
Cooking Time: 18 minutes
**DIFFICULTY LEVEL:** Easy
**SERVINGS:** 2

### INGREDIENTS
- Unsalted butter, 3 tbsp.
- Garlic cloves, minced, 4
- Chipotle chilies, chopped, 2 tsp.
- Orange juice, freshly squeezed, 1/2 cup
- Worcestershire sauce, 1/2 cup

- Cilantro, chopped, 3/4 cup
- Chicken breasts, skinless and boneless, 2 (cut into strips)
- Yellow mustard, 1 tsp.
- Salt and pepper, to taste
- Flour tortillas, 4-inch, 12
- Toppings: Shredded cabbage, lime wedges, salsa, sour cream, and cheese

## STEPS

1. In a skillet, melt butter over medium heat. Add garlic and chipotle, sautéing for about a minute.
2. Stir in orange juice, Worcestershire sauce, and half of the cilantro. Bring to a simmer.
3. Place the chicken strips in the skillet, cover, and cook over medium heat for about 13 minutes, turning halfway. Transfer to a plate and cover with foil.
4. Increase the heat, and reduce the sauce to about 1/4 cup, approximately 5 minutes.
5. Remove from heat, stir in mustard.
6. Shred the chicken using two forks and return it to the skillet.
7. Mix in the remaining cilantro, season with salt and pepper.
8. Assemble the tacos with chicken, shredded cabbage, lime wedges, salsa, sour cream, and cheese.

## NUTRITIONAL SERVING

Protein: 90g, Carbs: 44g, Fat: 20g, Sodium: 1600mg, Sugar: 14g, Potassium: 600mg.

**Recipe Tips:** For a smoky flavor, char the tortillas on an open flame before assembling the tacos.

## 7.10 Pork Schnitzel

Pork Schnitzel is a classic dish known for its crispy exterior and tender meat. It's a quick and delicious meal that is sure to satisfy.

**PREPARATION TIME:** 25 minutes

Cooking Time: 8 minutes

**DIFFICULTY LEVEL:** Hard

**SERVINGS:** 2

## INGREDIENTS

- Flour, 1/4 cup
- Salt, 1 tsp.
- Pepper, 1/4 tsp.
- Egg, 1
- Milk, 2 tbsp.
- Dry breadcrumbs, 3/4 cup
- Paprika, 1 tsp.
- Cooking spray
- Pork loin cutlets, 4 (thinly pounded)

## STEPS

1. Preheat air fryer to 375°F. Mix seasoned salt, pepper, and flour in one bowl. In another bowl, whisk together milk and egg. In a separate bowl, combine paprika and breadcrumbs.
2. Pound the pork cutlets to about a quarter-inch thickness. Dredge each cutlet in the flour mixture, shaking off excess. Then dip in the egg mixture, followed by the breadcrumb mixture, pressing to coat.
3. Place the breaded cutlets in the air fryer basket in a single layer. Spray lightly with cooking spray. Air fry for 4 minutes until lightly browned. Flip and spray again. Continue air frying for another 4 minutes until cooked through.
4. Serve the schnitzel with your choice of side dishes.

## NUTRITIONAL SERVING

Protein: 50g, Carbs: 20g, Fat: 11g, Sodium: 1200mg, Sugar: 14g, Potassium: 700mg.

**Recipe Tips:** For extra crispiness, let the breaded cutlets rest for 5 minutes before air frying.

## 7.11 Ravioli

These Air Fryer Ravioli offer a crispy, golden exterior with a savory beef filling, making them a delightful twist on the traditional Italian pasta dish. Ideal for those craving a unique and hearty appetizer.

**PREPARATION TIME:** 10 minutes
Cooking Time: 10 minutes
**DIFFICULTY LEVEL:** Easy
**SERVINGS:** 2

### INGREDIENTS
- Breadcrumbs, 1 cup
- Sliced Parmesan cheese, ¼ cup
- Dried basil, 2 tsp.
- Flour, ½ cup
- 2 large eggs, lightly beaten
- Beef ravioli, 9 ounces (fresh or pre-cooked)
- Chopped basil (for garnish)
- Cooking spray
- Marinara sauce, 1 cup (for serving)

### STEPS
1. Preheat air fryer to 350°F. In a bowl, combine breadcrumbs, parmesan cheese, and dried basil. Place flour and beaten eggs in separate bowls.
2. Coat each ravioli first in flour, then dip in the egg, and finally press into the breadcrumb mixture.
3. Arrange coated ravioli in a single layer on the air fryer tray sprayed with cooking oil. Air fry for 5 minutes, flip, spray again, and continue cooking for another 5 minutes until golden brown.
4. Serve with marinara sauce and garnish with chopped basil, if desired.

### NUTRITIONAL SERVING
Protein: 17g, Carb: 45g, Fat: 13g, Sodium: 23g, Sugar: 18g, Potassium: 16g.

**Recipe Tips:** For extra crispiness, let the coated ravioli sit for a few minutes before air frying.

## 7.12 Nashville Hot Chicken

Nashville Hot Chicken offers a fiery twist on traditional fried chicken. This spicy, tangy recipe brings the heat with a cayenne pepper-infused coating, perfectly contrasted with the coolness of pickles, making it a favorite for those who love bold and zesty flavors.

**PREPARATION TIME:** 25 minutes
Cooking Time: 14 minutes
**DIFFICULTY LEVEL:** Medium
**SERVINGS:** 2

### INGREDIENTS
- Dill pickle juice, 2 tsp.
- Spicy pepper sauce, 2 tsp.
- Salt, 1 tsp.
- Chicken tenderloins, 1 pounds
- Flour, 1 cup
- Mustard, ½ tsp.
- Buttermilk, ½ cup
- Egg, 1
- Cooking spray
- Cayenne pepper, 2 tsp.
- Brown sugar, 2 tbsp.
- Paprika, 1 tsp.
- Chili powder, 1 tsp.
- Garlic powder, ½ tsp.
- Dill pickle slices

### STEPS

1. Combine 2 teaspoons of spicy pepper sauce, 1/2 teaspoon of salt, and 2 teaspoons of dill pickle juice in a bowl. Add the chicken and place it in the fridge for about one hour. After marinating, drain the chicken, removing any excess marinade.
2. Preheat air fryer to 375°F. Combine the 1/2 teaspoon salt, pepper, and flour in a bowl. In a different bowl, combine buttermilk, egg, 1 tablespoon of spicy sauce, and 1 tablespoon of pickle juice. Dip the chicken in the flour to coat each side and shake off the excess. Then dip into the egg mixture, and finally dip again in the flour mixture.
3. Spray the chicken with vegetable oil and place it on the oiled tray in the basket of the air fryer. Air fry for about 7 minutes or until the color changes to a golden brown. Flip and apply the cooking spray. Air fry for a further 7 minutes or until lightly browned.
4. In a separate bowl, mix together 2 tablespoons of brown sugar, cayenne pepper, paprika, chili powder, and garlic powder. Sprinkle this mixture over the cooked chicken for the Nashville hot effect.

**NUTRITIONAL SERVING**
Protein: 39g, Carb: 21g, Fat: 20g, Sodium: 12g, Sugar: 9g, Potassium: 8g.

**Recipe Tips:** For an extra crispy coating, let the coated chicken sit for 10 minutes before air frying. This allows the coating to set and adhere better to the chicken.

# Chapter 7: Substitute Ingredients Guide

## 7.1 Bang Chicken

Vegetarian:
- Chicken: Replace with tofu or tempeh.

Gluten-Free:
- Flour: Use gluten-free all-purpose flour or almond flour.
- Sriracha sauce: Ensure it's gluten-free or substitute with a gluten-free hot sauce.

Allergen-Free:
- Egg: Use flaxseed meal (1 tbsp. flaxseed meal + 2.5 tbsp. water = 1 egg).
- Buttermilk: Use dairy-free milk mixed with 1 tsp. of lemon juice or vinegar.

## 7.2 Crispy Air Fryer Eggplant Parmesan

14. Vegetarian:
- Already vegetarian.

Gluten-Free:
- Wheat breadcrumbs: Use gluten-free breadcrumbs.
- Flour: Use gluten-free all-purpose flour.

Allergen-Free:
- Mozzarella cheese: Use dairy-free cheese.
- Parmesan cheese: Use vegan Parmesan or nutritional yeast.

## 7.3 Roasted Brussels Sprouts With Balsamic

Vegetarian: Already vegetarian.
Gluten-Free: Already gluten-free.
Allergen-Free: None required.

## 7.4 Chicken Nuggets

15. Vegetarian:
- Chicken breasts: Replace with tofu or seitan.

Gluten-Free:
- Panko: Use gluten-free panko breadcrumbs.

Allergen-Free:
- Parmesan: Use vegan Parmesan or nutritional yeast.

## 7.5 Dumplings

16. Vegetarian:

- Chicken dumplings: Use vegetable or tofu dumplings.

Gluten-Free:
- Ensure dumplings are gluten-free or use gluten-free alternatives.
- Soy sauce: Use tamari sauce or a gluten-free soy sauce.

Allergen-Free:
- Soy sauce: Use coconut aminos.

## 7.6 Pork Special Chops

17.
18. Vegetarian:
- Boneless pork: Substitute with seitan steaks or thick slices of tempeh.

Gluten-Free:
- Ensure grill seasoning is gluten-free or use individual gluten-free spices.

Allergen-Free:
- Dijon mustard: Check for allergens; some people are allergic to mustard.

## 7.7 Chicken Chimichangas

19.
20. Vegetarian:
- Rotisserie chicken: Replace with jackfruit, tofu, or beans.

Gluten-Free:
- Flour tortillas: Use gluten-free tortillas.

Allergen-Free:
- Ensure all products, especially store-bought salsa, are free from common allergens like nuts.

## 7.8 Simple Chicken Burrito Bowls

21.
22. Vegetarian:
- Rotisserie chicken: Use jackfruit, tofu, or beans.

Gluten-Free:
- Taco skillet sauce & Taco sauce: Ensure they are gluten-free or make your own.

Allergen-Free:
- Black beans: Some people are allergic; ensure it's okay or use another bean type.
- Sour cream: Use dairy-free sour cream.
- Cheddar cheese: Use dairy-free cheese.

## 7.9 Chicken Soft Tacos

Vegetarian:
- **Skinless and boneless chicken breasts**: Use firm tofu (pressed to remove excess water and marinated in the sauce), jackfruit, or store-bought vegetarian chicken substitutes. If using jackfruit, ensure it's young green jackfruit in water or brine, not in syrup.

Gluten-Free:
- **Worcestershire sauce**: Use a gluten-free version of Worcestershire sauce, available at health food or specialty stores.
- **Flour tortillas**: Replace with gluten-free tortillas, available at many grocery stores or health food stores.

Allergen-Free:
- **Unsalted butter**: Use a dairy-free margarine or olive oil.
- **Flour tortillas**: Replace with corn tortillas (make sure they don't have a wheat blend) or allergen-free tortillas.
- **Worcestershire sauce**: This sauce often contains fish (anchovies), so for a fish allergy, ensure you're using a vegan version.
- **Yellow mustard**: Some people might be allergic to mustard. You can skip it or use a small amount of vinegar for tanginess, but the flavor will be slightly different.

## 7.10    Pork Schnitzel

23. Vegetarian:
- **Pork sirloin cutlets**: Use seitan slices (wheat meat), tempeh slices, or store-bought vegetarian meat substitutes suitable for schnitzel.

Gluten-Free:
- **Flour**: Use gluten-free flour like chickpea flour, rice flour, or a gluten-free flour blend.
- **Dry breadcrumbs**: Use gluten-free breadcrumbs, available at many grocery stores or health food stores.

Allergen-Free:
- **Egg**: For the batter, you can create a flaxseed egg replacement (mix 1 tablespoon of ground flaxseed with 2.5 tablespoons of water, let it sit for 5 minutes to thicken).

- **Milk**: Use a lactose-free milk or non-dairy milk like almond, soy, or oat milk.
- **Cooking spray**: Make sure to use a cooking spray without allergens. Alternatively, you can lightly brush with a safe oil.
- **Pork**: As mentioned above in the vegetarian section, you can use seitan or tempeh, but ensure that these replacements are suitable for those with allergies, as seitan is made from wheat.

## 7.11 Ravioli
- Vegan:
  - Beef ravioli -> Vegan ravioli (filled with vegetables or vegan cheese)
- Gluten-Free:
  - Flour -> Gluten-free flour
  - Breadcrumbs -> Gluten-free breadcrumbs
  - Ravioli -> Gluten-free vegan ravioli
- Allergen-Free:
  - Eggs -> Chickpea flour (mix with water to create a batter)

## 7.12 Nashville Hot Chicken
- Vegan:
  - Tenderloin chicken -> Firm tofu, tempeh, or vegan chicken substitute
- Gluten-Free:
  - Flour -> Gluten-free all-purpose flour
- Allergen-Free:
  - Egg -> Flax egg (1 tbsp ground flaxseed + 2.5 tbsp water)
  - Buttermilk -> Plant-based milk with 1 tsp apple cider vinegar

Always ensure that the ingredient substitutes are safe for the individual's specific allergies, as individual reactions may vary. Checking labels on store-bought ite

# Chapter 8: Land Main Course Recipes

## 8.1 Loaded Pork Burritos

Loaded Pork Burritos offer a fusion of zesty and savory flavors, making them an irresistible choice. The combination of marinated pork, fresh salsa, and cheesy goodness wrapped in a soft tortilla creates a mouth-watering dish that's both filling and flavorful

http://tiny.cc/afca1

**PREPARATION TIME:** 25 minutes
Cooking Time: 8 minutes
**DIFFICULTY LEVEL:** Hard
**SERVINGS:** 2

**INGREDIENTS**
- Thawed limeade concentrate, ¾ cup
- Olive oil, 1 tbsp.
- Salt, 2 tsp.
- Pepper, 1 1/2 tsp.
- Boneless pork loin, 1-1/2 lbs, (sliced into thin pieces)
- Diced tomatoes (seeded), 1 cup
- Minced Green pepper, 1
- Minced onion, 1
- Minced cilantro, 1/4 cup
- Diced and seeded jalapeno pepper, 1
- Lime juice, 1 tsp.
- Garlic powder, 1/4 tsp.
- Uncooked rice (long-grain), 1 cup
- Shredded cheese (Monterey Jack), 3 cups
- Flour tortillas, 6
- Cleaned and drained black beans, 1 can (15 oz)
- Sour cream, 1-1/2 cups
- Cooking spray

**STEPS**

1. Mix the limeade concentrate, oil, 1 tsp. of salt, and 1 tsp. of pepper in a bowl. Coat the pork with this mixture, then cover and marinate for at least 20 minutes.
2. For the salsa, combine tomatoes, green pepper, onion, jalapeño, cilantro, lime juice, garlic powder, and the remaining salt and pepper in a separate bowl.
3. Cook the rice according to package instructions. Once cooked, stir in the remaining cilantro.
4. Remove the pork from the marinade and pat dry. Preheat the air fryer to 355°F. Spray the pork lightly with cooking spray and air fry in batches for about 8 minutes, flipping halfway through, until the pork is no longer pink.
5. Place 1/3 cup of cheese on each tortilla, then top with the pork, rice mixture, black beans, sour cream, and salsa. Serve with additional salsa on the side..

**NUTRITIONAL SERVING**
Protein: 35g, Carbs: 71g, Fat: 6g, Sodium: 1g, Sugar: 12g, Potassium: 5g.

**Recipe Tips:** For a more intense flavor, marinate the pork overnight in the refrigerator.

## 8.2 Sweet and Sour Pineapple Pork

Sweet and Sour Pineapple Pork is a delectable dish combining the sweetness of crushed pineapple with the tanginess of a rich sauce. Ideal for those who love the interplay of sweet and sour flavors.

**PREPARATION TIME:** 25 minutes
Cooking Time: 17 minutes
**DIFFICULTY LEVEL:** Hard
**SERVINGS:** 2

- Crushed unsweetened pineapple, 8 ounces
- Vinegar, 1/4 cup
- Sugar, 1/4 cup
- Brown sugar, 1/4 cup
- Ketchup, 1/4 cup
- Soy sauce, 1/2 cup
- Dijon mustard, 1 tbsp.
- Garlic, minced, 1 tsp.
- Pork tenderloins, 2 (approx. ¾ lb each)
- Salt, 1/4 tsp.
- Pepper, 1/4 tsp.
- Minced onions (for garnish)

## STEPS

1. Combine the first 8 ingredients in a skillet and cook on low heat. Whisk frequently and cook until it thickens, approximately 15 minutes.
2. Preheat the air fryer to 350°F. Season the pork with salt and pepper. Place pork in the air fryer basket on an oiled tray. Air fry for about 8 minutes until the pork edges begin to brown. Glaze the pork with the sauce. Continue air frying for about 9 minutes or until the internal temperature reaches 146°F. Let it rest for 5 minutes, then slice the pork. Serve with the spicy sauce and garnish with minced onions if desired.

## NUTRITIONAL SERVING

Protein: 35g, Carb: 71g, Fat: 6g, Sodium: 1g, Sugar: 12g, Potassium: 5g.

**Recipe Tips:** For a thicker sauce, mix a tablespoon of cornstarch with water and add to the sauce mixture before cooking.

## 8.3    Spicy Chicken Breasts

Spicy Chicken Breasts offer a tantalizing blend of hot and savory flavors, combining buttermilk's tenderness with a spicy crust. Ideal for those who enjoy a fiery kick in their meal.

**PREPARATION TIME:** 15 minutes
Cooking Time: 29 minutes
**DIFFICULTY LEVEL:** Easy
**SERVINGS:** 2

## INGREDIENTS
- Buttermilk, 2 cups
- Salt, 1 tsp.
- Breadcrumbs, 2 cups
- Dijon mustard, 1 tbsp.
- Hot pepper sauce, 1 tsp.
- Garlic powder, 1/2 tsp.
- Corn flour, 1 cup
- Chicken breast pieces, 8 ounces
- Canola oil, 1 tbsp.
- Poultry seasoning, 1/2 tsp.
- Mustard, 1/4 tsp.
- Paprika, 1/4 tsp.
- Cayenne pepper, 1/4 tsp.
- Oregano, 1/4 tsp.
- Dried parsley, 1/4 tsp.

## STEPS

1. Preheat air fryer to 375°F. In a mixing bowl, combine buttermilk, 1 tsp. salt, Dijon mustard, hot pepper sauce, and garlic powder. Submerge the chicken in the mixture, ensuring it's fully coated. Refrigerate for at least one hour.
2. In another bowl, mix corn flour, breadcrumbs, poultry seasoning, mustard, paprika, cayenne pepper, oregano, parsley, and remaining salt. Remove chicken from buttermilk mixture, allowing excess to drip off. Coat each piece in the breadcrumb mixture.
3. Place chicken in the air fryer basket on an oiled tray. Air fry for about 25 minutes, flipping halfway through, until the internal temperature reaches 170°F. For extra crispiness, air fry for an additional 4 minutes.

## NUTRITIONAL SERVING

Protein: 36g, Carb: 42g, Fat: 17g, Sodium: 8g, Sugar: 17g, Potassium: 9g.

**Recipe Tips:** Marinate the chicken overnight in the buttermilk mixture for enhanced flavor and tenderness.

## 8.4 Reuben Calzones

Reuben Calzones offer a creative twist on the classic Reuben sandwich, combining the delicious flavors of corned beef, Swiss cheese, and sauerkraut in a convenient, air-fried pastry.

**PREPARATION TIME:** 15 minutes
**Cooking Time:** 10 minutes
**DIFFICULTY LEVEL:** Medium
**SERVINGS:** 2

### INGREDIENTS
- Refrigerated pizza crust, 13.8 ounces
- Swiss cheese, 4 slices
- Sauerkraut, 1 cup, drained
- Cooked corned beef, ½ lb, chopped

### STEPS
1. Preheat air fryer to 400°F. Roll out the pizza crust on a lightly floured surface and shape it into a twelve-inch square. Cut into four equal squares.
2. On each square, place a slice of Swiss cheese, a portion of sauerkraut, and corned beef diagonally on one half. Fold the dough over the filling to form a triangle and press the edges with a fork to seal.
3. Place two calzones at a time in the air fryer basket on an oiled tray.
4. Air fry for about 10 minutes, turning halfway through, until they turn golden brown.
5. Serve hot with Thousand Island dressing or your preferred sauce.

### NUTRITIONAL SERVING
Protein: 21g, Carb: 49g, Fat: 17g, Sodium: 10g, Sugar: 11g, Potassium: 7g.

**Recipe Tips:** For a crisper crust, lightly brush the calzones with olive oil before air frying.

## 8.5 Steak with Garlic Herb Butter

Indulge in the rich and savory flavors of Steak with Garlic Herb Butter. This dish features a perfectly cooked sirloin steak, topped with a fragrant and buttery herb mixture, creating a delightful symphony of tastes.

**PREPARATION TIME:** 15 minutes
**Cooking Time:** 10 minutes
**DIFFICULTY LEVEL:** Medium
**SERVINGS:** 2

### INGREDIENTS
- Sirloin steak, 1 lb
- Butter, 4 tsp.
- Finely chopped parsley, 1 tsp.
- Chopped chives, 1 tbsp.
- Salt and black pepper, to taste
- Minced garlic clove, 1
- Crushed red pepper flakes, 1/4 tsp.

### STEPS
1. Allow the steak to rest at room temperature for about 30 minutes before cooking.
2. Preheat the air fryer to 400°F. Season the steak on both sides with a pinch of salt and black pepper. Place the steak in the center of the air fryer basket.
3. Cook for approximately 10 minutes, or until it reaches your desired doneness. Transfer the steak to a cutting board and let it rest for about 10 minutes.
4. Meanwhile, combine the parsley, butter, garlic, crushed red pepper, and chives in a bowl. Stir until well mixed.
5. Slice the steak across the grain into 1/4-inch-thick slices. Top with the garlic herb butter before serving.

### NUTRITIONAL SERVING

Protein: 47g, Carb: 1g, Fat: 64g, Sodium: 9g, Sugar: 0g, Potassium: 10g.

**Recipe Tips:** To enhance the flavor, allow the steak to come to room temperature before cooking, ensuring more even cooking and better flavor absorption.

## 8.6 Roast Chicken

Delight in the classic and comforting flavors of Roast Chicken. This simple yet elegant dish features a succulent, perfectly roasted chicken enhanced with herbs and spices, making it a timeless favorite for any meal.

**PREPARATION TIME:** 15 minutes
**Cooking Time:** 1 hour
**DIFFICULTY LEVEL:** Hard
**SERVINGS:** 2

**INGREDIENTS**
- Cooking spray
- Chicken, 3 pounds
- Olive oil, 1 tbsp.
- Fresh rosemary
- Black pepper ½ tsp
- Salt, 1 tsp
- Garlic, 8-12 cloves, minced
- Lemon, ½, juiced

**STEPS**
1. Preheat the air fryer to 375°F and coat the basket with non-stick cooking spray.
2. Rub the chicken with olive oil to tenderize the skin.

3. Season the chicken with salt and black pepper. Stuff the cavity with minced garlic, lemon juice, and rosemary. Place the chicken breast-side up in the air fryer basket, ensuring it doesn't touch the top of the fryer.
4. Air fry the chicken for approximately 1 hour, or until the thickest part of the thigh reaches an internal temperature of 165°F. The chicken should be golden brown and crispy.

**NUTRITIONAL SERVING**
Protein: 31g, Carbs: 3g, Fat: 28g, Sodium: 1400mg, Sugar: 1g, Potassium: 1100mg.

**Recipe Tips:** For added flavor, marinate the chicken with herbs and spices overnight in the refrigerator before roasting.

## 8.7 Mini Swedish Meatballs

Enjoy a taste of Scandinavia with these Mini Swedish Meatballs. Perfectly seasoned and air fried, they offer a delightful blend of flavors, making them a versatile dish that can be served as an appetizer or part of a main course.

**PREPARATION TIME:** 20 minutes
**Cooking Time:** 10 minutes
**DIFFICULTY LEVEL:** Easy
**SERVINGS:** 2

**INGREDIENTS**
- White bread slices, 2
- Milk, 1/4 cup
- Ground beef, 8 ounces
- Ground pork, 8 ounces
- Minced onion, ¼ cup
- Allspice, 1/2 tsp.
- Egg, 1
- Non-stick cooking spray
- Lingonberry jam (for serving)

- Black pepper and salt, to taste

STEPS

1. Soak the bread slices in milk for 5 minutes. Squeeze out the excess milk and tear the bread into small pieces. Place in a mixing bowl.
2. Add ground beef, ground pork, minced onion, allspice, salt, pepper, and egg to the soaked bread. Mix until well combined.
3. Form the mixture into small meatballs, each about the size of a heaped tablespoon.
4. Preheat the air fryer to 360°F. Spray the basket with cooking spray.
5. Place the meatballs in the basket, ensuring they are not overcrowded. Air fry for 10 minutes, shaking the basket halfway through, until the meatballs are browned and cooked through.
6. Serve with lingonberry jam.

NUTRITIONAL SERVING
Protein: 36g, Carbs: 14g, Fat: 14g, Sodium: 1200mg, Sugar: 15g, Potassium: 600mg.

**Recipe Tips:** For an authentic Swedish experience, serve these meatballs with a creamy sauce or over mashed potatoes.

## 8.8 Za'atar Lamb Chops

Delight in the aromatic and savory taste of Za'atar Lamb Chops. These chops are seasoned with a blend of za'atar and other spices, then air-fried to perfection, offering a juicy and flavorful experience.

PREPARATION TIME: 20 minutes
**Cooking Time:** 10 minutes (5 minutes per side)
DIFFICULTY LEVEL: Hard
SERVINGS: 2

INGREDIENTS

- Bone-in lamb loin chops, 8 (each weighing around 3 ½ ounces)
- Crushed garlic cloves, 3
- Extra-virgin olive oil, 1 tbsp.
- Lemon juice, 1 tsp.
- Za'atar, 1 tbsp.
- Salt, 1/2 tsp.
- Ground black pepper

STEPS

1. Rub the lamb chops with olive oil and crushed garlic.
2. Sprinkle lemon juice on both sides of the chops. Season with za'atar, salt, and black pepper.
3. Preheat the air fryer to 400°F. Place the lamb chops in the air fryer basket in batches, ensuring they are not overcrowded.
4. Air fry for 5 minutes on one side. Flip the chops and continue air frying for another 5 minutes or until the desired level of doneness is achieved.
5. Serve hot, garnished with additional za'atar or fresh herbs if desired.

NUTRITIONAL SERVING
Protein: 69g, Carbs: 12g, Fat: 13g, Sodium: 1500mg, Sugar: 19g, Potassium: 1200mg.

**Recipe Tips:** For a more intense flavor, marinate the lamb chops with za'atar and olive oil for an hour before air frying.

## 8.9 Meatballs

Enjoy the classic and comforting taste of homemade Meatballs, perfectly seasoned and air-fried for a healthier alternative. These meatballs are juicy, flavorful, and great for a variety of dishes.

PREPARATION TIME: 30 minutes

**Cooking Time:** 10 minutes (8 minutes initial cooking + 2 minutes additional cooking)

**DIFFICULTY LEVEL:** Hard

**SERVINGS:** 2

## INGREDIENTS

- Ground beef, 16 ounces
- Ground pork, 4 ounces
- Italian seasoning, 1 tsp.
- Salt, 1/2 tsp.
- Garlic cloves, minced, 2
- Grated Parmesan cheese, 1/2 cup
- Egg, beaten, 1
- Italian seasoned breadcrumbs, 1/2 cup

## STEPS

1. Preheat the air fryer to 350°F.
2. In a mixing bowl, combine ground beef, ground pork, Italian seasoning, salt, minced garlic, Parmesan cheese, beaten egg, and breadcrumbs. Mix well.
3. Form the mixture into 16 meatballs using an ice cream scoop or your hands.
4. Place the meatballs in the air fryer basket, ensuring they are not overcrowded. Cook for 8 minutes.
5. After 8 minutes, check the meatballs and cook for an additional 2 minutes if necessary.
6. Once cooked, transfer the meatballs to a plate and repeat the process with any remaining mixture.

## NUTRITIONAL SERVING

Protein: 29g, Carbs: 31g, Fat: 10g, Sodium: 1200mg, Sugar: 13g, Potassium: 1000mg.

**Recipe Tips:** For an added depth of flavor, consider mixing a small amount of red wine into the meat mixture before forming the meatballs.

# Chapter 8: Substitute Ingredients Guide

## 8.1 Loaded Pork Burritos:

Vegetarian:
- Boneless pork loin: Replace with thinly sliced seitan or portobello mushrooms. **Gluten-Free:**
- Flour tortillas: Use gluten-free tortillas. **Allergen-Free:**
- Shredded cheese (Monterey Jack): Use dairy-free cheese or skip.
- Whipped cream: Use dairy-free sour cream or skip.

## 8.2 Sweet and Sour Pineapple Pork:

Vegetarian:
- Pork tenderloins: Replace with tofu or tempeh. **Gluten-Free:**
- Soy sauce: Use gluten-free soy sauce or tamari. **Allergen-Free:**
- Soy sauce: Use coconut aminos.

## 8.3 Spicy Chicken Breasts:

Vegetarian:
- Chicken breast pieces: Replace with firm tofu or seitan slices. **Gluten-Free:**
- Breadcrumbs: Use gluten-free breadcrumbs. **Allergen-Free:**
- Buttermilk: Use almond milk with a splash of lemon juice or vinegar.
- Mustard: Skip or replace with a mustard-free blend.

## 8.4 Reuben Calzones:

Vegetarian:
- Cooked corned beef: Replace with seitan or marinated tofu. **Gluten-Free:**
- Refrigerated pizza crust: Use gluten-free pizza crust. **Allergen-Free:**
- Swiss cheese: Use dairy-free cheese or skip.

## 8.5 Steak with Garlic Herb Butter:

Vegetarian:
- Sirloin steak: Replace with portobello mushrooms or a thick slice of seitan. **Gluten-Free:** Already gluten-free. **Allergen-Free:**
- Butter: Use dairy-free butter or olive oil.

## 8.6 Roast Chicken:

Vegetarian:
- Chicken: Replace with a whole roasted cauliflower or tofu block. **Gluten-Free:** Already gluten-free. **Allergen-Free:** Already allergen-free.

## 8.7 Mini Swedish Meatballs:

Vegetarian:
- Beef and Pork: Use a blend of lentils, breadcrumbs, and mushrooms to make vegetarian meatballs. **Gluten-Free:**
- White bread slices: Use gluten-free bread. **Allergen-Free:**
- Milk: Use almond milk or another dairy-free alternative.
- Egg: Use a flaxseed or chia seed egg replacement.

## 8.8 Za'atar Lamb Chops

Vegetarian:
- All trimmed bone-in lamb loin chops: Substitute with firm tofu or tempeh, cut into similar size pieces. You can also use Portobello mushrooms as a meaty substitute. Make sure to marinate in the same spices and herbs to infuse flavor.

Gluten-Free:
- No adjustments needed for this recipe.

Allergen-Free:
- Crushed garlic cloves: Omit or replace with a pinch of asafoetida powder for a similar flavor.
- Extra-virgin olive oil: Replace with any preferred allergen-free oil.
- Lemon: Some people might be allergic to citrus; in such cases, omit or use a splash of apple cider vinegar for a hint of tanginess.

## 8.9 Meatballs

Vegetarian:
- Ground leaf & Ground pork: Substitute with an equal amount of a mixture of cooked lentils, mushrooms, and ground walnuts or use ready-made vegetarian meat substitutes available in the market.

Gluten-Free:
- Italian seasoned breadcrumbs: Replace with gluten-free breadcrumbs or almond meal.

Allergen-Free:
- Garlic cloves: Omit or replace with a pinch of asafoetida powder.
- Parmesan cheese: Use dairy-free cheese or nutritional yeast for a cheesy flavor.
- Egg: Use a flax egg (1 tbsp ground flaxseed mixed with 2.5 tbsp water and let sit for 5 minutes).

# Chapter 9: Seafood First Course Recipes

## 9.1 Shrimp Fajitas

Shrimp Fajitas combine bold and vibrant flavors of shrimp with colorful bell peppers and sweet onions, all wrapped in warm tortillas. This dish is perfect for a quick and tasty meal, offering an ideal balance of flavor and nutrition.

**PREPARATION TIME:** 30 minutes
**Cooking Time:** 6-8 minutes
**DIFFICULTY LEVEL:** Hard
**SERVINGS:** 2

### INGREDIENTS
- Shrimp, 1 pound
- Green bell pepper, 1, thinly sliced
- Red bell pepper, 1, thinly sliced
- Sweet onion, 1/2 cup, thinly sliced
- Gluten-free fajita seasoning, 2 tablespoons
- Olive oil, 2 tablespoons
- Flour tortillas, 6

### STEPS
1. Lightly coat the air fryer basket with olive oil.
2. Pat the shrimp dry and season with half of the gluten-free fajita seasoning.
3. In a mixing bowl, toss the shrimp, sliced bell peppers, and onion with olive oil and the remaining fajita seasoning.
4. Place the shrimp and vegetable mixture in the air fryer basket in a single layer.
5. Air fry at 390°F for about 6-8 minutes, or until the shrimp are cooked through and the vegetables are tender.
6. Serve the cooked shrimp and vegetables on warm flour tortillas.

### NUTRITIONAL SERVING
Protein: 48g, Carbohydrates: 40g, Fat: 15g, Sodium: 700mg, Sugars: 8g, Potassium: 600mg, Calories: ~500 kcal.

**Recipe Tips:** For a more intense flavor, marinate the shrimp in fajita seasoning for at least 30 minutes before cooking.

## 9.2 Honey Glazed Air Fryer Salmon

Indulge in the delectable Honey Glazed Air Fryer Salmon, where the natural richness of salmon meets a sweet and savory honey glaze. This easy-to-prepare dish is perfect for a quick yet elegant meal, offering a balanced combination of flavors that will delight seafood lovers.

**PREPARATION TIME:** 15 minutes
**Cooking Time:** 8 minutes
**DIFFICULTY LEVEL:** Easy
**SERVINGS:** 2

### INGREDIENTS
- Salmon fillets, 4
- Black pepper
- Salt
- Soy sauce, 2 tsp.
- Honey, 1 tbsp.
- Sesame seeds, 1 tsp.

### STEPS
1. Preheat the air fryer to 375°F.
2. Season the salmon fillets with salt and pepper. Brush each fillet with soy sauce.
3. Place the fillets in the air fryer basket and cook for 8 minutes.

4. During the last minute of cooking, brush the fillets with honey and sprinkle with sesame seeds.

**NUTRITIONAL SERVING**
Protein: 45g, Carbs: 15g, Fat: 27g, Sodium: 480mg, Sugar: 12g, Calories: 500.

**Recipe Tips:**
To ensure an even glaze, apply honey using a pastry brush and cook the salmon skin-side down to retain its moisture and tenderness.

## 9.3 Fish Tacos

Fish Tacos blend the fresh taste of the sea with vibrant citrus and creamy textures, creating a delightful meal that's both satisfying and light.

**PREPARATION TIME:** 15 minutes
**Cooking Time:** 8 minutes
**DIFFICULTY LEVEL:** Easy
**SERVINGS:** 2

**INGREDIENTS**
- Firm white fish fillets, 24 oz
- Grill pepper seasoning, 1 tbsp.
- Avocado, 1
- Oranges, 2
- Red onion, 1/4 cup
- Fresh coriander, 2 tbsp.
- Salt, 1 tsp.
- Mayonnaise, 1/4 cup
- Chipotle sauce, 1/4 cup
- Lime juice, 1 tbsp.
- Corn tortillas, 6

**STEPS**
- In a bowl, mix diced avocado, orange segments, half of the salt, and cilantro to create a citrus salsa.

- In a separate bowl, blend mayonnaise, chipotle sauce, the remaining salt, and lime juice for a spicy mayonnaise sauce.
- Season the fish evenly with grill pepper seasoning.
- Lightly oil the air-fryer basket to prevent sticking.
- Place fish in the basket in a single layer. Air fry at 400°F for about 8 minutes until the internal temperature of the fish reaches 145°F.
- To assemble the tacos, place a portion of fish on each corn tortilla, top with the spicy mayonnaise, and finish with the citrus salsa.

**NUTRITIONAL SERVING**
Protein: 25g, Carb: 30g, Fat: 14g, Sodium: 1700mg, Sugar: 23g, Potassium: 1200mg, Calories: Approx. 300-350 kcal per serving

**Recipe Tips:** For a crunchier texture, briefly grill the corn tortillas on an open flame before assembling the tacos.

## 9.4 Shrimp

Indulge in the simple yet flavorful delight of Shrimp, where the sweetness of the shrimp is enhanced by a blend of lemon, honey, and garlic. This easy-to-make dish is perfect for a quick, delicious meal that's both light and satisfying.

**PREPARATION TIME:** 15 minutes
**Cooking Time:** 7 minutes
**DIFFICULTY LEVEL:** Easy
**SERVINGS:** 2

**INGREDIENTS**
- Shrimp, 1 lb, peeled and deveined
- Olive oil, 1 ½ tsp.
- Lemon juice, 1 ½ tsp.

- Honey, 1 ½ tsp.
- Chopped garlic, 2 cloves
- Salt, 1/8 tsp.
- For garnishing: Sliced lime wedges, fresh cilantro

## STEPS

1. In a bowl, whisk together olive oil, lemon juice, honey, chopped garlic, and salt to create a marinade.
2. Add the shrimp to the marinade, ensuring they are well-coated. Let them marinate for at least 10 minutes.
3. Preheat air fryer to 395°F.
4. Place the shrimp in the air fryer basket in a single layer, shaking off any excess marinade.
5. Air fry the shrimp for approximately 7 minutes at 370°F, shaking the basket once halfway through, until they are pink and slightly golden.
6. Serve the shrimp garnished with lime slices and fresh cilantro.

## NUTRITIONAL SERVING

Protein: 23g, Carbs: 32g, Fat: 23g, Sodium: 15mg, Sugar: 14g, Potassium: 9mg, Calories: Approx. 300 kcal.

**Recipe Tips:** To ensure even cooking, don't overcrowd the air fryer basket. Arrange the shrimp in a single layer and cook in batches if necessary.

## 9.5 Teriyaki Salmon Fillets with Broccoli

Savor the fusion of Asian flavors with these Teriyaki Salmon Fillets accompanied by tender broccoli. This dish combines the richness of salmon with a sweet and savory teriyaki glaze, balanced by the freshness of lightly air-fried broccoli, making it a nutritious and flavorful meal.

**PREPARATION TIME:** 20 minutes

**Cooking Time:** 9 minutes
**DIFFICULTY LEVEL:** Easy
**SERVINGS:** 2

## INGREDIENTS

- Broccoli florets, 2 cups
- Olive oil, 2 tsp.
- Soy sauce, 1 tbsp.
- Salt and black pepper, to taste
- Sugar, 1 tsp.
- Vinegar, 1 tsp.
- Cornstarch, 1/4 tsp.
- Minced ginger, 1 1/2-inch piece
- Salmon fillets, two 6-ounce pieces
- Sliced scallions, for garnish
- Cooked white rice, for serving

## STEPS

1. Toss broccoli florets with 1 tsp. of olive oil. Season with salt and pepper. Place in the air fryer basket.
2. In a small bowl, combine soy sauce, sugar, vinegar, cornstarch, and ginger. Mix well to create the teriyaki sauce.
3. Brush salmon fillets with the remaining olive oil. Then, generously apply the teriyaki sauce on top of each fillet.
4. Place the salmon fillets on top of the broccoli in the air fryer basket, skin-side down.
5. Air fry at 390°F for 9 minutes or until the broccoli is tender and the salmon is fully cooked.
6. Serve the salmon and broccoli on plates, garnished with sliced scallions. Accompany with cooked white rice.

## NUTRITIONAL SERVING

Protein: 37g, Carbs: 57g, Fat: 20g, Sodium: 15g, Sugar: 12g, Potassium: 7g, Calories: 500 kcal.

## Recipe Tips:

To enhance the flavor, let the salmon marinate in the teriyaki sauce for about 30 minutes before cooking.

## 9.6 Fried Shrimp

Indulge in the crispy delight of Fried Shrimp, a classic favorite made healthier in the air fryer. These shrimps are coated in a light, crunchy layer of panko breadcrumbs, delivering a satisfying crunch with every bite. Paired with a fiery remoulade sauce, it's a perfect blend of flavor and texture.

**PREPARATION TIME:** 10 minutes
**Cooking Time:** 10 minutes
**DIFFICULTY LEVEL:** Easy
**SERVINGS:** 2

**INGREDIENTS**
- Nonstick cooking spray
- Shrimp, 1 lb, peeled and deveined
- Salt and black pepper, to taste
- Eggs, 2, beaten
- Panko breadcrumbs, 1 cup
- Fiery remoulade sauce:
- Mayonnaise, ½ cup
- Minced jalapenos, 2 tsp.
- Mustard, 2 tsp.
- Ketchup, 1 tbsp.
- Chili sauce, 1 tbsp.
- Finely chopped scallion, 1

**STEPS**
1. Spray the air fryer basket with cooking spray. Pat the shrimp dry with paper towels and season with salt and pepper.
2. In one bowl, place beaten eggs. In another bowl, place the panko breadcrumbs.
3. Dip each shrimp into the egg, allowing excess to drip off. Then coat in the panko breadcrumbs.
4. Preheat the air fryer to 420°F. Place the shrimp in the basket in a single layer, lightly spraying them with cooking spray.
5. Air fry for 10 minutes, turning the shrimp halfway through, until golden brown.
6. For the remoulade sauce, combine mayonnaise, jalapenos, mustard, ketchup, chili sauce, and scallion in a bowl. Mix until smooth.

**NUTRITIONAL SERVING**
Protein: 10g, Carbs: 12g, Fat: 0g, Sodium: 12g, Sugar: 15g, Potassium: 6g, Calories: 240 kcal.

**Recipe** **Tips:**
To prevent the breadcrumbs from falling off, let the coated shrimp rest for a few minutes before air frying.

## 9.7 Salmon with Maple-Dijon Glaze

This "Salmon with Maple-Dijon Glaze" recipe offers a delightful balance of sweet and tangy flavors, enveloping the rich and tender salmon fillets in a luscious glaze. Ideal for a quick yet elegant meal, the dish combines the natural succulence of salmon with a flavorful glaze that's sure to impress.

**PREPARATION TIME:** 10 minutes
**Cooking Time:** 6 minutes
**DIFFICULTY LEVEL:** Easy
**SERVINGS:** 2

**INGREDIENTS**
- Salmon fillets, 4 ounces each
- Butter, 3 tbsp.
- Maple syrup, 3 tbsp.
- Dijon mustard, 1 tbsp.
- Lemon juice, from 1 lemon
- Garlic clove, minced, 1
- Olive oil, 1 tbsp.
- Salt, 1/4 tsp.
- Pepper, 1/4 tsp.

**STEPS**
1. Preheat the air fryer to 400°F.

2.  In a small saucepan, melt the butter over medium heat. Add maple syrup, Dijon mustard, minced garlic, and lemon juice. Reduce the heat and simmer for 3 minutes until the mixture thickens.
3.  Lightly brush the salmon fillets with olive oil and season with salt and pepper. Place the fillets in the air fryer basket.
4.  Air fry the salmon for approximately 6 minutes or until it reaches the desired doneness and has a light golden color.
5.  Generously glaze the salmon with the maple-Dijon mixture before serving.

## NUTRITIONAL SERVING

Protein: 19g, Carbs: 11g, Fat: 23g, Sodium: 7g, Sugar: 11g, Potassium: 4g, Calories: 280 kcal.

**Recipe Tips:** For a deeper infusion of flavors, marinate the salmon in the glaze for 30 minutes before cooking.

# Chapter 9: Substitute Ingredients Guide

## 9.1 Shrimp Fajitas
Vegetarian:
- Shrimp: Substitute with firm tofu or tempeh, seasoned and air fried.
- Flour tortillas: Ensure they are vegetarian (some might contain lard).

Gluten-Free:
- Flour tortillas: Substitute with gluten-free tortillas.

Allergen-Free:
- Gluten-free fajita: Ensure it doesn't contain any allergens relevant to the consumer.

## 9.2 Honey Glazed Air Fryer Salmon
Vegetarian:
- Salmon fillets: Substitute with seasoned and air-fried firm tofu or tempeh.

Gluten-Free:
- Soy sauce: Substitute with tamari or gluten-free soy sauce.

Allergen-Free:
- Soy sauce: Use a soy-free alternative like coconut aminos.

## 9.3 Fish Tacos
Vegetarian:
- Firm white fish fillets: Substitute with seasoned and air-fried firm tofu or tempeh.

Gluten-Free:
- Corn tortillas: Ensure they are gluten-free as some might contain traces of gluten.

Allergen-Free:
- Mayonnaise: Ensure it doesn't contain any allergens relevant to the consumer or use an allergen-free brand.

## 9.4 Shrimp
Vegetarian:
- Shrimp: Substitute with seasoned and air-fried firm tofu or tempeh.

Gluten-Free:
- No substitutions required.

Allergen-Free:

- Check the components of any pre-made seasoning or sauce for potential allergens.

## 9.5 Teriyaki Salmon Fillets with Broccoli
Vegetarian:
- Salmon fillets: Substitute with seasoned and air-fried firm tofu or tempeh.

Gluten-Free:
- Soy sauce: Substitute with tamari or gluten-free soy sauce.

Allergen-Free:
- Soy sauce: Use a soy-free alternative like coconut aminos.

## 9.6 Fried Shrimp
Vegetarian:
- Shrimps: Substitute with firm tofu or tempeh, seasoned and coated with the same breadcrumb mixture.

Gluten-Free:
- Panko breadcrumbs: Substitute with gluten-free panko or breadcrumbs.
- Ensure other sauces and condiments used are gluten-free.

Allergen-Free:
- Panko breadcrumbs: Use allergen-free breadcrumbs.
- Check the components of any pre-made seasoning, sauces, or condiments for potential allergens.

## 9.7 Salmon with Maple-Dijon Glaze
Vegetarian:
- Salmon fillets: Substitute with seasoned and air-fried firm tofu or tempeh.

Gluten-Free:
- No substitutions required.

Allergen-Free:
- Check the components of any pre-made seasoning or sauce for potential allergens.

Note: Always check the labels of any store-bought ingredients to ensure they don't contain hidden allergens. Different brands might have different ingredients or processing methods.

# Chapter 10: Seafood Main Course Recipes

## 10.1 Fish and Fries

Fish and Fries is a classic pairing that delivers the delicate, flaky textures of haddock with the fulfilling crunch of homemade fries. This dish offers a delightful blend of tastes and textures, perfect for those who appreciate traditional seafood with a cozy side.

**PREPARATION TIME:** 20 minutes
**Cooking Time:** 17 minutes
**DIFFICULTY LEVEL:** Hard
**SERVINGS:** 2

**INGREDIENTS**
- Potatoes, 1 pound
- Olive oil, 2 tbsp.
- Pepper, 1/4 tsp.
- Salt, 1/4 tsp.
- Flour, 1/3 cup (gluten-free if necessary)
- Egg (or egg replacer), 1
- Water, 2 tbsp.
- Cornflakes (gluten-free), 2/3 cup
- Parmesan cheese (or vegan alternative), 1 tbsp.
- Cayenne Pepper, 1/8 tsp.
- Haddock (or tofu for vegan), 1 pound

**STEPS**
1. Preheat the air fryer to 400 °F. Peel and slice the potatoes into half-inch thick sticks.
2. Toss the potato sticks with olive oil, salt, and pepper. Place them in the air fryer basket in a single layer and cook for about 8 minutes until soft and golden brown.
3. In a bowl, mix flour and pepper. In another bowl, whisk together the egg and water. In a third bowl, combine cornflakes, Parmesan cheese, and cayenne pepper.
4. Season the fish with salt. Dip in the flour mixture, followed by the egg mixture, and then coat with the cornflake mixture.
5. Remove the fries from the air fryer. Place the fish in the basket and cook for about 9 minutes, turning halfway through.
6. Reheat the fries in the basket if necessary. Serve immediately with tartar sauce if desired.

**NUTRITIONAL SERVING**
Protein: 89g, Carbs: 40g, Fat: 15g, Sodium: 24g, Sugar: 29g, Potassium: 21g

**Recipe Tips:** For extra crispy fries, soak the cut potatoes in cold water for at least 30 minutes before air frying. This step helps remove excess starch, resulting in crispier fries.

## 10.2 Popcorn Shrimp Tacos with Cabbage Slaw

Savor the crunch and zest with Popcorn Shrimp Tacos, a delightful combination of crispy shrimp and refreshing cabbage slaw, all wrapped in a soft tortilla. This dish brings a playful twist to classic tacos, perfect for a quick and satisfying meal.

**PREPARATION TIME:** 15 minutes
**Cooking Time:** 6 minutes
**DIFFICULTY LEVEL:** Medium
**SERVINGS:** 2

**INGREDIENTS**
- Coleslaw mix, 2 cups
- Fresh cilantro, 1/4 cup, chopped
- Lime juice, 2 tbsp

- Honey, 2 tbsp
- Salt, 1/4 tsp
- Eggs, 2
- Milk, 2 tbsp
- All-purpose flour, 1/2 cup
- Panko breadcrumbs, 1-1/2 cups
- Ground cumin, 1 tbsp
- Garlic powder, 1 tbsp
- Raw shrimp, 1 pound, peeled and deveined
- Corn tortillas, 8
- Cooking spray
- Ripe avocado, 1, sliced

## STEPS

1. In a bowl, mix coleslaw, cilantro, lime juice, honey, and salt. Set aside for the slaw.
2. In a separate bowl, whisk together eggs and milk. Place flour in another bowl. Combine panko, cumin, and garlic powder in a third bowl.
3. Dredge shrimp in flour, shaking off excess. Dip in egg mixture, then coat with panko mix, pressing to adhere.
4. Spray air fryer basket with cooking spray. Place shrimp in a single layer on the tray.
5. Air fry at 375°F for about 6 minutes, flipping halfway, until shrimp are golden and cooked.
6. Warm tortillas as per preference.
7. Assemble tacos with shrimp, avocado slices, and coleslaw.

## NUTRITIONAL SERVING

Protein: 48g, Carbs: 58g, Fat: 22g, Sodium: 680mg, Sugar: 14g, Potassium: 632mg, Calories: Approx. 700 kcal.

**Recipe Tips:** To keep the shrimp crispy, air fry just before assembling the tacos and serve immediately.

## 10.3 Bacon Wrapped Scallops

Experience the sumptuous taste of Bacon Wrapped Scallops, where the sweetness of the scallops meets the smoky flavor of bacon. This dish is a perfect blend of flavors and textures, making it an elegant yet simple choice for any occasion.

**PREPARATION TIME:** 15 minutes
**Cooking Time:** 8 minutes
**DIFFICULTY LEVEL:** Easy
**SERVINGS:** 2

## INGREDIENTS

- Sea scallops, 16, medium-sized
- Bacon, 8 slices, cut in half crosswise
- Freshly ground black pepper
- Olive oil, for brushing
- Toothpicks, 16

## STEPS

1. Preheat the air fryer to 400°F.
2. Partially cook the bacon in the air fryer for about 3 minutes, flipping once. It should be flexible, not crisp. Remove and drain on paper towels.
3. Dry the scallops with paper towels and remove the small muscle on the side if attached.
4. Wrap each scallop with a piece of bacon and secure with a toothpick. Brush lightly with olive oil and season with black pepper.
5. Place scallops in a single layer in the air fryer basket.
6. Air fry for about 8 minutes, turning halfway, until scallops are opaque and bacon is crispy.

## NUTRITIONAL SERVING

Protein: 24g, Carbs: 3g, Fat: 7g, Sodium: 558mg, Sugar: 0g, Potassium: 356mg, Calories: Approx. 200 kcal.

**Recipe Tips:** For a more pronounced flavor, marinate the scallops in a mixture of olive oil, lemon juice, and garlic before wrapping them in bacon.

## 10.4 Cajun Shrimp

taste of the South to your table. This recipe combines succulent shrimp with a blend of Cajun spices and colorful vegetables for a meal that's as visually appealing as it is delicious.

**PREPARATION TIME:** 20 minutes

**DIFFICULTY LEVEL:** Medium

**SERVINGS:** 2

**INGREDIENTS**

- Jumbo shrimp, 1 lb, peeled and deveined
- Cajun or Creole seasoning, 1 tbsp.
- Zucchini, 1, sliced
- Yellow squash, 8 oz, sliced
- Red bell pepper, 1, sliced
- Salt, ¼ tsp.
- Olive oil, 2 tsp.

**STEPS**

1. In a bowl, toss the shrimp with Cajun seasoning until evenly coated.
2. In another bowl, combine zucchini, yellow squash, red bell pepper, salt, and olive oil, mixing well.
3. Preheat the air fryer to 400°F.
4. In batches, arrange the shrimp and vegetables in the air fryer basket, ensuring they are not overcrowded. Air fry for about 10 minutes, shaking the basket several times during cooking for even frying.
5. Repeat with the remaining shrimp and vegetables.
6. Once all batches are cooked, return the first batch to the air fryer and heat for an additional minute.

**NUTRITIONAL SERVING**

Protein: 23g, Carbs: 18g, Fat: 7g, Sodium: 870mg, Sugar: 6g, Potassium: 630mg, Calories: Approx. 210 kcal.

**Recipe Tips:** For an extra kick, add a splash of hot sauce or a squeeze of lemon juice to the shrimp before serving.

## 10.5 Salmon Patties

Experience the delightful and savory taste of Salmon Patties, a dish that combines the richness of salmon with fresh herbs and spices. These patties are not only delicious but also offer a healthy and satisfying meal.

**PREPARATION TIME:** 15 minutes

**Cooking Time:** 15 minutes

**DIFFICULTY LEVEL:** Easy

**SERVINGS:** 2

**INGREDIENTS**

- Mayonnaise, ½ cup
- Minced garlic, 1 tsp.
- Lemon juice, ½ tsp.
- Cajun seasoning, 2 pinches
- Salmon, 12 ounces, drained and flaked
- Fresh chives, 1 tbsp., chopped
- Dried parsley, 1 tsp.
- Salt, ½ tsp.
- Minced garlic, ½ tsp.
- All-purpose flour, 1 tbsp.
- Cooking spray
- Lemon, for garnish

**STEPS**

1. In a small bowl, mix mayonnaise, minced garlic, Cajun seasoning, and lemon juice. Refrigerate until needed.
2. In a medium mixing bowl, combine salmon, chives, parsley, salt, and additional minced garlic. Add flour and mix thoroughly.
3. Divide the mixture into four equal parts and shape into patties.
4. Preheat the air fryer to 350°F (175°C). Cut the lemon into four wedges.
5. Place salmon patties over lemon slices at the bottom of the air fryer basket. Lightly spray the patties with cooking spray.

6. Reduce the temperature to 275°F (135°C) and air fry for 15 minutes or until the internal temperature of a patty reaches 145°F (63°C). Serve with the prepared sauce.

**NUTRITIONAL SERVING**
Protein: 22g, Carbs: 11g, Fat: 9g, Sodium: 430mg, Sugar: 1g, Potassium: 380mg, Calories: Approx. 200 kcal.

**Recipe Tips:** Add a bit of lemon zest to the salmon mixture for a brighter flavor.

## 10.6 Salmon with Wholegrain Mustard Glaze

Savor the rich and flavorful Salmon with Wholegrain Mustard Glaze. This dish features tender salmon fillets glazed with a savory mix of mustard and herbs, creating a delightful balance of flavors.

**PREPARATION TIME:** 16 minutes
**Cooking Time:** 10 minutes
**DIFFICULTY LEVEL:** Easy
**SERVINGS:** 2

**INGREDIENTS**
- Salmon fillets, 2
- Salt and black pepper, to taste
- Olive oil, 2 tsp.
- Wholegrain mustard, 2 tbsp.
- Brown sugar, 1 tbsp.
- Minced garlic clove, 1
- Thyme leaves, ½ tsp.

**STEPS**
1. Season salmon fillets with salt and pepper.
2. In a small bowl, mix wholegrain mustard, brown sugar, olive oil, thyme, and minced garlic. Apply this mixture generously over the salmon.

3. Place the salmon fillets in the air fryer basket.
4. Air fry at 400°F for 9–10 minutes, or until the salmon is cooked to your liking and the glaze is slightly caramelized.

**NUTRITIONAL SERVING**
Protein: 23g, Carbs: 12g, Fat: 13g, Sodium: 320mg, Sugar: 7g, Potassium: 500mg, Calories: Approx. 250 kcal.

**Recipe Tips:** For a crisper glaze, broil the salmon for the last 2 minutes of cooking.

## 10.7 Healthy Fish Finger Sandwich and Optimum Healthy Air Fry

Enjoy a healthier twist on the classic fish finger sandwich with this recipe, featuring crispy air-fried fish fingers paired with a tangy pea puree. A delicious and nutritious take on a beloved comfort food.

http://tiny.cc/afsea6
**PREPARATION TIME:** 15 minutes
Cooking Time: 15 minutes
**DIFFICULTY LEVEL:** Easy

**SERVINGS:** 2

**INGREDIENTS**
- Small cod fillets, 4
- Salt and pepper, to taste
- Flour, 2 tbsp.
- Dry breadcrumbs, 40 g
- Olive oil spray
- Frozen peas, 250 g
- Crème fraiche, 1 tbsp.
- Capers, 10-12, drained
- Lemon juice, to taste
- Bread rolls, 4

**STEPS**
1. Preheat the air fryer.
2. Lightly coat each fish fillet with flour and season with salt and pepper. Cover evenly with breadcrumbs for a thin, crispy layer.
3. Spray the air fryer basket with olive oil. Add the cod fillets and cook on the fish setting (200°C) for 15 minutes.
4. While the fish cooks, boil the peas briefly until tender. Blend the peas with crème fraiche, capers, and lemon juice to create a smooth puree.
5. Assemble the sandwiches with the bread rolls, air-fried fish, and pea puree. Add other toppings like lettuce or tartar sauce if desired.

**NUTRITIONAL SERVING**
Protein: 25g, Carbs: 35g, Fat: 9g, Sodium: 400mg, Sugar: 5g, Potassium: 300mg, Calories: Approx. 350 kcal.

**Recipe Tips:** Add a dash of paprika to the breadcrumb mix for an extra flavor kick

# GET YOUR BONUSES NOW!

**Effortless Air Fryer Meal Prep For Health Enthusiast**

Download your free bonus meal prep guidebook now!

## Scan the QR Code and Get the Bonus

## https://bit.ly/airfryerlanding

# Chapter 10: Substitute Ingredients Guide

## 10.1 Fish and Fries:
Vegetarian:
- Haddock: Replace with a vegetarian fish substitute available at stores (like Gardein Fishless Filet) or firm tofu seasoned similarly.

Gluten-Free:
- Flour: Replace with gluten-free flour or almond flour.
- Cornflakes: Ensure they are gluten-free or use gluten-free breadcrumbs.

Allergen-Free:
- Egg: Use a flaxseed egg (1 tbsp. ground flaxseed + 2.5 tbsp. water) or a commercial egg replacer.
- Parmesan cheese: Omit or use a dairy-free cheese alternative.

## 10.2 Popcorn Shrimp Tacos with Cabbage Slaw:
Vegetarian:
- Non-cooked shrimp: Use a vegetarian shrimp substitute available in stores or marinated firm tofu cubes.

Gluten-Free:
- Flour: Replace with gluten-free flour.
- Panko breadcrumbs: Use gluten-free breadcrumbs.

Allergen-Free:
- Eggs: Use a flaxseed egg or commercial egg replacer.
- Milk: Use a non-dairy milk like almond or oat milk.

## 10.3 Bacon Wrapped Scallops:
Vegetarian:
- Sea scallops: Use king oyster mushroom stems.
- Sliced bacon centrally: Use vegetarian bacon or thinly sliced tofu marinated in liquid smoke and soy sauce.

**Gluten-Free**: No substitutions necessary.

**Allergen-Free**: No substitutions necessary.

## 10.4 Cajun Shrimp:
Vegetarian:

- 24 jumbo shrimps: Use vegetarian shrimp substitutes available in stores or marinated firm tofu cubes.

**Gluten-Free**: No substitutions necessary.

**Allergen-Free**: No substitutions necessary.

## 10.5 Salmon Patties:
Vegetarian:
- Salmon: Use mashed chickpeas or another bean variety.

Gluten-Free:
- Flour: Replace with gluten-free flour.

Allergen-Free:
- Mayonnaise: Use egg-free mayonnaise.

## 10.6 Salmon:
Vegetarian:
- Salmon fillets: Use a vegetarian salmon substitute available at stores or marinated and grilled firm tofu slices.

**Gluten-Free**: No substitutions necessary.

**Allergen-Free**: No substitutions necessary.

## 10.7 Healthy Fish Finger Sandwich and Optimum Healthy Air Fry:
Vegetarian:
- Tiny cod fillets: Use a vegetarian fish substitute available at stores (like Gardein Fishless Sticks) or use firm tofu sticks seasoned similarly.

Gluten-Free:
- Flour: Replace with gluten-free flour.
- Dry breadcrumbs: Use gluten-free breadcrumbs.
- Bread rolls: Ensure they are gluten-free or use gluten-free bread.

Allergen-Free:
- Crème fraiche: Use a dairy-free alternative or omit.

Remember to always check the labels when buying processed or packaged foods to ensure they meet your dietary requirements. If any other allergens need to be addressed (like nuts or soy), please let me know

# Chapter 11: Side Dishes Recipes

## 11.1 Pakoras

Pakoras are a delightful Indian snack, famous for their crisp texture and savory flavor. This version, made with cauliflower and potatoes, offers a healthier twist by air-frying instead of deep-frying.

**PREPARATION TIME:** 15 minutes
**Cooking Time:** 16 minutes
**DIFFICULTY LEVEL:** Easy
**SERVINGS:** 2

### INGREDIENTS
- Cauliflower, sliced, 2 cups
- Potatoes, diced, 1 cup
- Chickpea flour, 1 1/4 cups
- Water, 3/4 cup
- Red onion, chopped, 1/2 tbsp
- Salt, 1 tbsp
- Garlic, minced, 1 clove
- Curry powder, 1 tsp
- Cilantro, chopped, 1 tsp
- Cayenne pepper, 1/2 tsp
- Cumin, 1/2 tsp
- Cooking spray

### STEPS
1. In a large mixing bowl, combine cauliflower, potatoes, chickpea flour, water, red onion, garlic, curry powder, cayenne, cumin, cilantro, and salt. Let it rest for 10 minutes.
2. Preheat air fryer to 180°C.
3. Apply cooking spray to the air fryer basket. Half-fill the basket with the cauliflower mixture and spread evenly. Avoid overcrowding.
4. Air fry for 8 minutes, then flip and continue air frying for another 8 minutes. Place on a plate lined with paper towels. Repeat with remaining batter.

**NUTRITIONAL SERVING**
Protein: 17g, Carbs: 3g, Fat: 15g, Sodium: 2g, Sugar: 2g, Potassium: 3g, Calories: Approx. 200 kcal.

**Recipe Tips:** Serve hot with a side of mint or tamarind chutney for an authentic Indian snack experience.

## 11.2 Loaded Greek Fries

Loaded Greek Fries combine the crispiness of air-fried potatoes with the freshness of Greek-inspired toppings. This dish is perfect for those who love the fusion of flavors, offering a delicious and visually appealing side.

**PREPARATION TIME:** 10 minutes
**Cooking Time:** 15 minutes
**DIFFICULTY LEVEL:** Easy
**SERVINGS:** 2

### INGREDIENTS
- Cucumber, 1/2 small, finely grated
- Salt, 1/2 tsp.
- Greek yogurt, 6 ounces
- Lemon juice, 1 tbsp.
- Dill (freeze-dried), 2 tsp.
- Garlic (minced), 1 tsp.
- Vinegar, 1 tsp.
- Feta cheese (crumbled), 4 ounces
- Russet potatoes (medium-sized), 4, cut into fries
- Olive oil, 2 tsp.
- Greek seasoning, 2 tsp.

- Cooking spray
- Red onion (sliced into strips), 1 small
- Kalamata olives (sliced), 1/4 cup
- Grape tomatoes (halved), 12

**STEPS**

1. Salt the grated cucumber and let it drain in a sieve for 10 minutes.
2. In a small bowl, mix Greek yogurt, lemon juice, dill, garlic, vinegar, and feta. Stir until combined. Add the cucumber just before serving.
3. Preheat air fryer to 450°F.
4. Toss fries with olive oil and Greek seasoning. Spray the air fryer basket with cooking spray and add half the fries.
5. Air fry for 10 minutes, then flip and cook for an additional 5 minutes. Repeat with the remaining fries.
6. Serve the fries topped with tzatziki sauce, red onion strips, Kalamata olives, and grape tomatoes.

**NUTRITIONAL SERVING**

Protein: 11g, Carbs: 47g, Fat: 14g, Sodium: 620mg, Sugar: 6g, Fiber: 3g, Calories: ~350 kcal.

**Recipe Tips:** For extra crispiness, ensure the fries are not overcrowded in the air fryer basket.

## 11.3 Fingerling Potatoes with Dip

These Fingerling Potatoes with Dip are a delightful side dish, featuring crispy potatoes paired with a creamy and tangy dipping sauce. Perfect for a comforting yet elegant addition to any meal.

http://tiny.cc/afsid7
**PREPARATION TIME:** 10 minutes
**Cooking Time:** 18-30 minutes
**DIFFICULTY LEVEL:** Easy

**SERVINGS:** 2
**INGREDIENTS**
- Fingerling potatoes, 12 ounces
- Olive oil, 1 tbsp
- Garlic powder, 1 tsp
- Paprika, 1/4 tsp
- Salt and pepper to taste

Sauce:
- Sour cream, 1/3 cup
- Mayonnaise, 2 ounces
- Finely grated Parmesan cheese, 2 tsp
- Ranch dressing mix, 1 ½ tsp
- White vinegar, 1 tbsp
- Chopped fresh parsley, 1 tbsp

**STEPS**

1. Preheat the air fryer to 395°F.
2. Toss the potatoes with olive oil, garlic powder, paprika, salt, and pepper in a bowl.
3. Transfer the seasoned potatoes to the air fryer basket.
4. Air fry for 18-30 minutes, shaking the basket halfway through, until the potatoes are well cooked and crispy.
5. While the potatoes are cooking, mix sour cream, mayonnaise, ranch dressing mix, Parmesan cheese, and vinegar in a small bowl.
6. Serve the air-fried potatoes on a plate, sprinkled with parsley, and accompanied by the prepared dipping sauce.

**NUTRITIONAL SERVING**

Protein: 7g, Carbs: 36g, Fat: 24g, Sodium: 200mg, Sugar: 2g, Potassium: 300mg, Calories: Approx. 300-350 kcal per serving.

**Recipe Tips:** For extra crispiness, ensure the potatoes are not overcrowded in the air fryer basket and are evenly coated with oil.

## 11.4 Loaded Cheese and Onion Fries

Loaded Cheese and Onion Fries bring a delicious twist to classic fries. Topped with tangy feta, crisp onions, and olives, these fries are a perfect blend of flavors and textures, making them an irresistible side dish.

**PREPARATION TIME:** 10 minutes
**Cooking Time:** 15 minutes
**DIFFICULTY LEVEL:** Easy

SERVINGS: 2

INGREDIENTS

- Cucumber, 1/2 small
- Salt, 1/2 tsp
- Greek yogurt, 6 ounces
- Lemon juice, 1 tbsp
- Dried dill, 2 tsp
- Garlic, minced, 1 tsp
- Vinegar, 1 tsp
- Feta cheese, crumbled, 4 ounces
- Russet potatoes, 4, medium-sized
- Olive oil, 2 tsp
- Greek seasoning, 2 tsp
- Cooking spray
- Red onion, sliced into strips, 1 small
- Kalamata olives, sliced, 1/4 cup
- Grape tomatoes, halved, 12

STEPS

1. Shred and salt the cucumber. Place in a sieve for 10 minutes to drain.
2. Mix Greek yogurt, lemon juice, dill, garlic, vinegar, and feta cheese in a bowl. Stir until combined. Add cucumber when ready to use.
3. Preheat the air fryer to 450°F.
4. In a large bowl, toss the potatoes with olive oil and Greek seasoning. Spray air fryer tray with nonstick cooking oil and place half of the fries in the basket.
5. Air fry for 10 minutes, flip, and cook for an additional 5 minutes or until crispy. Repeat with the remaining fries.
6. Serve the fries, topped with tzatziki sauce, red onion strips, Kalamata olives, and grape tomatoes.

NUTRITIONAL SERVING

Protein: 10g, Carbs: 17g, Fat: 15g, Sodium: 200mg, Sugar: 2g, Potassium: 300mg, Calories: Approx. 300-350 kcal per serving.

**Recipe Tips:** For best results, ensure the fries are evenly spaced in the air fryer to cook uniformly.

# 11.5 Paneer Pakoras

Paneer Pakoras offer a delightful vegetarian treat, combining the richness of paneer with aromatic spices in a crispy chickpea flour batter. These bites are a perfect fusion of Indian flavors and are great as a snack or side dish.

**PREPARATION TIME:** 15 minutes
**Cooking Time:** 16 minutes
**DIFFICULTY LEVEL:** Medium
**SERVINGS:** 2

INGREDIENTS

- Cauliflower, sliced, 2 cups
- Potatoes, diced, 1 cup
- Paneer (Indian cottage cheese), cubed, 1 cup
- Chickpea flour, 1 1/4 cups
- Water, 3/4 cup
- Red onion, chopped, 1/2 tbsp
- Salt, 1 tbsp
- Garlic, minced, 1 clove
- Curry powder, 1 tsp
- Cilantro, chopped, 1 tsp
- Cayenne pepper, 1/2 tsp
- Cumin, ground, 1/2 tsp
- Cooking spray

STEPS

1. Mix cauliflower, potatoes, paneer, chickpea flour, water, red onion, garlic, curry powder, cilantro, cayenne pepper, cumin, and salt in a large bowl. Let the mixture rest for 10 minutes.
2. Preheat the air fryer to 356°F (180°C).
3. Coat the air fryer basket with cooking spray. Half-fill the basket with the mixture and smooth out. Avoid overcrowding.
4. Air fry for 8 minutes, flip, and cook for another 8 minutes. Place on a plate lined with paper towels. Repeat with the remaining batter.

NUTRITIONAL SERVING

Protein: 6.1g, Carbs: 0.3g, Fat: 6g, Sodium: 200mg, Sugar: 2g, Potassium: 300mg, Calories: Approx. 180-220 kcal per serving.

**Recipe Tips:** For extra crispiness, ensure the pakoras are not touching each other in the air fryer basket.

## 11.6 Pork B Apple Crisp alls

Pork Balls offer a savory and satisfying bite, perfect for a hearty appetizer or side dish. These balls, made with a blend of pork and spices, then glazed with a sweet and tangy sauce, provide a delightful mix of flavors and textures.

**PREPARATION TIME:** 10 minutes
**Cooking Time**: 15-20 minutes
**DIFFICULTY LEVEL:** Hard
**SERVINGS:** 2

**INGREDIENTS**
- Quick cooking oats, 2/3 cup
- Ritz crackers, crushed, 1/2 cup
- Eggs, beaten, 2
- Milk, 5 ounces
- Onion, minced, 1 tbsp
- Salt, 1 tsp
- Garlic, minced, 1 tsp
- Ground cumin, 1 tsp
- Honey, 1 tsp
- Mustard, 1/2 tsp
- Ground pork, 2 pounds

For sauce
- Brown sugar, 1/3 cup
- Honey, 1/3 cup
- Orange marmalade, 1/3 cup
- Cornstarch, 2 tsp
- Soy sauce, 2 tsp
- Louisiana-style hot sauce, 1-2 tsp
- Worcestershire sauce, 1 tbsp

**STEPS**
1. Set the air fryer to 380°F. Mix the first 10 ingredients in a large bowl. Gently incorporate the ground pork. Form into 1 to 1.25-inch balls.

2. Place the pork balls in a single layer on a greased tray in the air fryer basket. Cook for 14-15 minutes or until cooked through and browned.
3. Meanwhile, combine sauce ingredients in a small saucepan. Cook and stir briefly until thickened.

**NUTRITIONAL SERVING**
Protein: 6.1g, Carbs: 0.3g, Fat: 6.7g, Sodium: 200mg, Sugar: 2g, Potassium: 300mg, Calories: Approx. 200-250 kcal per serving.

**Recipe Tips:** For an extra tangy taste, let the pork balls marinate in the sauce for a few minutes before serving.

## 11.7 Southern Cheese

This Southern Cheese sandwich is a delightful twist on the classic grilled cheese, featuring the added richness of a fried egg and crispy bacon. It's a hearty and satisfying meal, perfect for breakfast or a comforting lunch.

**PREPARATION TIME:** 1 min
Cooking Time: 10 minutes
**DIFFICULTY LEVEL:** Easy
**SERVINGS:** 2

**INGREDIENTS**
- Bread slices, 2
- Eggs, 1
- Cheese slices, 2 (e.g., cheddar or American)
- Bacon pieces, 2
- Mayonnaise, 1/2 tbsp
- Butter, up to 1/2 tbsp

**STEPS**
1. Cook the bacon in the air fryer at 380°F for about 3 minutes, or until crispy.
2. Meanwhile, heat a skillet and lightly toast the bread slices with a bit of butter.
3. Fry the eggs in the skillet, flipping them halfway to ensure even cooking on both sides.
4. Place a slice of cheese on one slice of toasted bread. Top it with a fried egg and crispy bacon.
5. Add another slice of cheese on top of the bacon, then cover with the second slice of toasted bread.

6. Place the assembled sandwich back into the air fryer and cook for about 2 minutes, or until the cheese is melted and the sandwich is heated through.

**NUTRITIONAL SERVING**
Protein: 23g, Carbs: 30g, Fat: 27g, Sodium: 750mg, Sugar: 3g, Fiber: 2g.

**Recipe Tips:** For a healthier version, use whole grain bread, low-fat cheese, and turkey bacon.

## 11.8  Pumpkin Fries

Pumpkin Fries present a delightful twist on traditional fries, offering a sweet and savory experience with a hint of spice. These are a perfect fall treat or a healthier alternative to regular potato fries, packing a flavorful punch with each bite.

**PREPARATION TIME:** 25 minutes
Cooking Time: 8 minutes
**DIFFICULTY LEVEL:** Medium
**SERVINGS:** 2
**INGREDIENTS**
- Greek yogurt, 1/2 cup
- Maple syrup, 2 tablespoons
- Chopped chipotle peppers, 3 teaspoons
- Salt, 1/8 teaspoon
- A small pumpkin approximately 1-2 pounds suitable for cutting into fries.
- Garlic powder, 1/4 teaspoon
- Ground cumin, 1/4 teaspoon
- Chili powder, 1/4 teaspoon
- Pepper, 1/4 teaspoon

**STEPS**
1. Combine the maple syrup, chipotle peppers, salt, and yogurt in a shallow bowl. Place it in the fridge until ready to eat.

2. Preheat the air fryer to 402°F. Cut and peel a small pumpkin in half lengthwise. Remove the seeds. Slice the pumpkin into quarter-inch-wide strips, resembling fries. Toss the strips with cumin, pepper, salt, chili powder, and garlic powder.
3. Place the seasoned pumpkin strips on a greased tray in the air fryer basket. Air fry for about eight minutes until they turn golden brown and crispy.

**NUTRITIONAL SERVING**
Protein: 5g, Carbs: 31g, Fat: 3g, Sodium: 200mg, Sugar: 10g, Potassium: 300mg.

**Recipe Tips:** For evenly cooked fries, make sure to cut the pumpkin into uniform strips and do not overcrowd the air fryer basket.

## 11.9  Fried Rice with Sesame Sriracha Sauce

Experience a unique twist on the classic fried rice with this Sesame Sriracha Sauce version. This dish combines the aromatic flavors of sesame with the heat of Sriracha, enhancing the simple yet delightful taste of fried rice.

**PREPARATION TIME:** 15 minutes
**Cooking Time:** 14 minutes
**DIFFICULTY LEVEL:** Easy
**SERVINGS:** 2

**INGREDIENTS**
- Cooked white rice, 2 cups
- Olive oil, 1 tbsp.
- Toasted sesame oil, 2 tsp.
- Sriracha, 1 tsp.
- Soy sauce, 1 tsp.

- Salt and black pepper, to taste
- Sesame seeds, 1/2 tsp.
- Egg, 1
- Mixed vegetables (carrots and peas), 1 cup

## STEPS

1. In a bowl, mix rice with olive oil, 1 tbsp. water, and sesame oil. Season with salt and pepper.
2. Transfer the rice mixture to a metal or foil pan suitable for your air fryer size.
3. Air fry at 350°F for 14 minutes, stirring halfway through.
4. Meanwhile, mix sriracha, soy sauce, 1 tsp. sesame oil, and sesame seeds in a separate bowl.
5. Fry an egg in the air fryer, covered, for 4 minutes or until cooked to your preference.
6. Add the carrots and peas to the rice. Continue air frying, covered, for an additional 2 minutes.
7. Serve the fried rice topped with the egg and drizzled with the Sesame Sriracha sauce.

## NUTRITIONAL SERVING

Protein: 15g, Carbs: 78g, Fat: 14g, Sodium: 620mg, Sugar: 6g, Fiber: 3g.

**Recipe Tips:** For added crunch, garnish with extra sesame seeds or sliced green onions before serving.

# Chapter 11: Substitute Ingredients Guide

## 11.1 Pakoras:
Vegetarian:
- No substitutions needed. All ingredients are vegetarian. **Gluten-Free:**
- Chickpea flour: Ensure it's gluten-free or use a gluten-free flour blend. **Allergen-Free:**
- Chickpea flour: Some people allergic to legumes might be allergic to chickpeas. Substitute with rice flour.

## 11.2 Loaded Greek Fries:
Vegetarian:
- No substitutions needed. All ingredients are vegetarian. **Gluten-Free:**
- Ensure Greek seasoning is gluten-free. **Allergen-Free:**
- Greek yogurt: Use dairy-free yogurt (e.g., coconut or almond-based yogurt).
- Cheese box (crumbled feta): Use dairy-free feta.

## 11.3 Fingerling Potatoes with Dip: Vegetarian:
- No substitutions needed as provided. Ensure further ingredients are vegetarian. **Gluten-Free:**
- Ensure further ingredients are gluten-free. **Allergen-Free:**
- Will need the full recipe to recommend allergen-free substitutions.

## 11.4 Loaded Cheese and Onion Fries Vegetarian:
No substitutions needed as the recipe is already vegetarian.
Gluten-Free:
- Replace **Greek seasoning** with a gluten-free variant or make your own mix at home with spices like oregano, thyme, basil, rosemary, and marjoram.

Allergen-Free:
- Replace **Greek yogurt** with dairy-free yogurt (e.g. coconut yogurt or almond yogurt).
- Replace **Feta cheese** with dairy-free feta cheese or tofu crumbles marinated in lemon juice and salt.

## 11.5 Paneer Pakoras Vegetarian:
No substitutions needed as the recipe is already vegetarian.
Gluten-Free:
- Use a gluten-free **cooking spray** or simply use a brush with oil for the air fryer basket.

Allergen-Free:
- Replace **Cheese** with dairy-free cheese or tofu.
- Ensure the **cooking spray** is free from allergens specific to the individual's needs.

## 11.6 Pork Balls
Vegetarian:
- Replace **Pork** with a mixture of mashed beans (e.g., black beans, chickpeas), breadcrumbs, and vegetables (like mushrooms, bell peppers) for a vegetarian meatball alternative.

Gluten-Free:
- Replace **Ritz crackers** with gluten-free breadcrumbs or almond meal.
- Replace **Oats for quick cooking** with certified gluten-free oats.
- For the sauce, ensure the **soy sauce** is gluten-free or replace with tamari.
- Check the **Worcestershire sauce** for gluten; opt for a gluten-free variant if needed.

Allergen-Free:
- For those allergic to soy, replace **soy sauce** with coconut aminos.
- Ensure the **Worcestershire sauce** is free from allergens specific to the individual's needs or skip it.
- Use dairy-free milk in place of regular **milk**.

## 11.7 Southern Cheese
- **Vegan**: Substitute "Bacon pieces" with vegan bacon or tofu slices, "Cheese slices" with vegan cheese, and "Butter" with vegan butter. Use egg-free mayonnaise.
- **Gluten-Free**: Replace "Bread slices" with "Gluten-free bread".
- **Allergen-Free**: Use egg-free mayonnaise and vegan cheese.

## 11.8 Pumpkin Fries
- Vegan:
  - Greek yogurt -> Vegan yogurt (coconut or almond)
- Gluten-Free:
  - Ensure that all ingredients used are gluten-free
- Allergen-Free:
  - Greek yogurt -> Vegan yogurt (coconut or almond)

## 11.9 Fried Rice with Sesame Sriracha Sauce:

Vegetarian: Already vegetarian. Gluten-Free:

- Soya sauce: Use gluten-free soy sauce or tamari.

  **Allergen-Free:**

- Egg: Skip or replace with diced tofu.

- Soya sauce: Use coconut aminos.

# Chapter 12: Vegetarian Recipes

## 12.1 Veggie Chip Medley

Veggie Chip Medley is a colorful and healthy snack made from a variety of vegetables. These chips are a great way to enjoy the flavors of different vegetables in a fun and crunchy form

**PREPARATION TIME:** 14 minutes
**Cooking Time:** 16 minutes
**DIFFICULTY LEVEL:** Hard
**SERVINGS:** 2

### INGREDIENTS
- Sweet potato, 4 ounces
- Purple potato, 4 ounces
- Olive oil, 2 tbsp
- Black pepper and salt
- Red beet, 1
- Golden beet, 1

### STEPS
1. Wash and dry the vegetables thoroughly. Slice them into 1/4 inch thick pieces.
2. Toss the potato slices with olive oil, salt, and pepper.
3. Preheat the air fryer to 350°F. Place the potato slices in the basket in a single layer, cooking them for 8 minutes, flipping halfway through, until they are golden brown.
4. In another bowl, toss the beet slices with olive oil, salt, and a pinch of crushed red pepper.
5. Combine the potato and beet chips in a bowl with a pinch of salt. Store in a container once cooled.

### NUTRITIONAL SERVING
Protein: 10g, Carbs: 1g, Fat: 11g, Sodium: 200mg, Sugar: 2g, Potassium: 300mg, Calories: Approx. 130 kcal per serving.

**Recipe Tips:** For an extra crisp texture, ensure the vegetables are thoroughly dried before frying.

## 12.2 Twice Air Fried Vegan Stuffed Idaho Potatoes

Experience a delightful twist on the classic baked potato with these Twice Air Fried Vegan Stuffed Idaho Potatoes. This recipe turns ordinary potatoes into a creamy, flavorful, and satisfying meal, with a crispy skin and a soft, flavorful interior, perfect for a comforting vegan dish

**PREPARATION TIME:** 15 minutes
**Cooking Time:** 50-60 minutes
**DIFFICULTY LEVEL:** Hard
**SERVINGS:** 2

### INGREDIENTS
- Large potatoes, 2
- Olive oil, 1 - 2 tsp.
- Unsweetened vegan yogurt, ¼ cup
- Vegan milk, ¼ cup
- Nutritional yeast, 2 tsp.
- Salt, ½ tsp.
- Pepper, ¼ tsp.
- Minced spinach, 1 cup

For topping
- Unsweetened vegan yogurt, ¼ cup
- Salt and pepper (smoked)
- Parsley chives (chopped)

### STEPS
- Spray the potatoes with oil on both sides.
- Preheat your air fryer at 380 degrees. Once preheated, add the potatoes.
- Cook the potatoes for 40-50 minutes or until tender, flipping them halfway through the cooking process.
- Let the potatoes cool enough to handle safely.
- Slice each potato in half lengthwise. Carefully scoop out the center, leaving a thin layer of potato inside the skin.
- Mash the scooped potato with nutritional yeast, vegan yogurt, pepper, and salt.
- Mix in the minced spinach. Refill the potato shells with this mixture.

- Cook the stuffed potatoes again for 5-10 minutes at 325 °F.

**NUTRITIONAL SERVING**

Protein: 2g, Carb: 20g, Fat: 8g, Sodium: 2g, Sugar: 2g, Potassium: 3g, Calories: Approx. 200-250 kcal per serving.

**Recipe**                                **Tips:**

For an extra crispy skin, brush the outside of the potatoes with a bit more olive oil before the final air frying step.

## 12.3 Potato Chips

Crispy and light, these homemade Potato Chips are a healthier alternative to store-bought snacks. Air-fried to perfection, they offer a delightful crunch with just a hint of sea salt.

**PREPARATION TIME:** 35 minutes
**Cooking Time:** 15-17 minutes
**DIFFICULTY LEVEL:** Hard
**SERVINGS:** 2

**INGREDIENTS**

- Large potatoes, 2
- Olive oil spray
- Sea salt, ½ tsp.

**STEPS**

1. Preheat the air fryer to 360 °F.
2. Use a mandolin or vegetable peeler to slice the potatoes very thinly. Soak them in a bowl of cold water for 15 minutes, then rinse and soak again for another 15 minutes.
3. Drain and dry the potato slices on towels. Spray them with cooking spray and sprinkle with sea salt.

4. Place batches of potato slices on the greased air fryer basket tray, lightly coating each batch. Cook until crisp and lightly browned, about 15-17 minutes, turning and tossing every 6 minutes.

**NUTRITIONAL SERVING**

Protein: 99g, Carb: 50g, Fat: 25g, Sodium: 2g, Sugar: 2g, Potassium: 3g, Calories: Approx. 300-350 kcal per serving.

**Recipe**                                **Tips:**

For extra flavor, experiment with different seasonings like smoked paprika or garlic powder.

## 12.4 Radishes

Enjoy a unique twist on radishes with this air-fried recipe. These radishes turn into a delightful snack or side dish, acquiring a crispy texture and enhanced flavor with a touch of oregano.

**PREPARATION TIME:** 21 minutes
**Cooking Time:** 15 minutes
**DIFFICULTY LEVEL:** Hard
**SERVINGS:** 2

**INGREDIENTS**

- Radishes, 2-1/4 pounds
- Olive oil, 3 tbsp.
- Oregano, 1 tbsp.
- Salt, 1/4 tsp.
- Pepper, 1/8 tsp.

**STEPS**

1. Preheat the air fryer to 375 °F.
2. In a bowl, thoroughly mix the radishes with olive oil, oregano, salt, and pepper.

3. Place the seasoned radishes on an oiled tray in the air fryer basket. Fry for about 15 minutes, stirring occasionally, until crispy.

**NUTRITIONAL SERVING**
Protein: 80g, Carb: 45g, Fat: 22g, Sodium: 2g, Sugar: 2g, Potassium: 3g, Calories: Approx. 300-350 kcal per servin
Recipe Tips:
To add a bit of zest, sprinkle some lemon juice over the radishes before serving.

## 12.5 General Tso's Cauliflower

Savor the bold flavors of General Tso's Cauliflower, a vegetarian twist on the classic dish. Crispy air-fried cauliflower florets are tossed in a sweet and spicy sauce, offering a deliciously satisfying meal.

**PREPARATION TIME:** 20 minutes
**Cooking Time:** 10-12 minutes
**DIFFICULTY LEVEL:** Hard
**SERVINGS:** 2

**INGREDIENTS**
- Flour, 1/2 cup.
- Cornstarch, 1/2 cup.
- Salt, 1 tsp.
- Baking powder, 1 tsp.
- Club soda, 3/4 cup.
- Head cauliflower (medium), 1
**For the Sauce:**
  - Water, 1/3 cup
  - Balsamic vinegar, 1/3 cup
  - Soy sauce, 2 tsp
  - Honey, 2 tsp
  - Chili sauce, 2 tsp
  - Minced garlic cloves, 2
  - Water, 1 tsp
  - Cornstarch, 1 tsp

**For Garnish:**
- Sliced green onions

**STEPS**
1. Preheat the air fryer to 400°F.
2. In a large bowl, mix flour, cornstarch, salt, and baking powder. Add club soda right before frying. Toss the cauliflower florets in the batter and let rest on a rack for 5 minutes.
3. Place battered cauliflower in a greased air fryer basket. Cook until soft and lightly browned, about 10-12 minutes.
4. For the sauce, combine balsamic vinegar, garlic, water, chili sauce, soy sauce, and honey in a skillet over medium heat. Bring to a low boil and cook until reduced, about 15 minutes.
5. Mix 1 tsp of water with cornstarch and add to the sauce to thicken.
6. Toss the crispy cauliflower in the sauce. Serve with rice and garnish with sliced green onions.

**NUTRITIONAL SERVING**
Protein: 15g, Carb: 6g, Fat: 4g, Sodium: 2g, Sugar: 2g, Potassium: 3g, Calories: Approx. 200-250 kcal per serving.

**Recipe Tips:**
For an extra crunch, sprinkle toasted sesame seeds on top before serving.

## 12.6 Green Tomato Stacks

Green Tomato Stacks offer a delightful twist on the traditional BLT. Layered with crispy green tomatoes, bacon, and lettuce, these stacks provide a unique blend of flavors and textures, perfect for a light and satisfying meal.

**PREPARATION TIME:** 20 minutes
**Cooking Time:** 8-12 minutes
**DIFFICULTY LEVEL:** Hard
**SERVINGS:** 2

**INGREDIENTS**
- Mayonnaise, 1/4 cup
- Lime zest, 1/4 tsp
- Lime juice, 2 tbsp

- Thyme, 1 tsp
- Pepper, 1/2 tsp
- Flour, 1/4 cup
- Large egg whites, 2
- Cornmeal, 3/4 cup
- Salt, 1/4 tsp
- Green tomatoes, 2 (medium)
- Red tomatoes, 2 (medium)
- Cooking spray
- Canadian bacon slices, 8

## STEPS

1. Preheat air fryer to 375°F. In a bowl, combine mayonnaise, lime zest, lime juice, thyme, and pepper. Refrigerate until ready to use.
2. Set up three shallow dishes: one with flour, one with beaten egg whites, and one with cornmeal mixed with salt and remaining pepper.
3. Slice each tomato into four pieces crosswise. Lightly coat each slice with flour, dip in egg whites, then in the cornmeal mixture.
4. Spray tomatoes with cooking spray and place them in batches on a tray in the air fryer basket. Cook for 4-6 minutes until lightly browned. Flip, spray again, and cook for another 4-6 minutes until golden brown.
5. Assemble each stack with a slice of bacon, a green tomato slice, and a red tomato slice. Drizzle with the prepared mayo mixture.

## NUTRITIONAL SERVING

Protein: 12g, Carb: 14g, Fat: 3g, Sodium: 2g, Sugar: 2g, Potassium: 3g, Calories: Approx. 180-220 kcal per serving.

## Recipe Tips:

For an extra crunch, add a sprinkle of crumbled feta cheese on top of the stacks before serving.

## 12.7 Cumin Carrots

Cumin Carrots bring a delightful combination of earthy and slightly spicy flavors, making them a perfect side dish. The roasting process enhances the natural sweetness of the carrots, while cumin adds a warm depth, creating a delicious and healthy accompaniment to any meal.

**PREPARATION TIME:** 20 minutes
**Cooking Time:** 12-15 minutes
**DIFFICULTY LEVEL:** Hard
**SERVINGS:** 2

## INGREDIENTS

- Coriander seeds, 2 tsp
- Cumin seeds, 2 tsp
- Carrots, 1 pound, cut into sticks
- Coconut oil, 1 tbsp
- Garlic, 2 cloves, minced
- Salt, 1/4 tsp
- Pepper, 1/8 tsp
- Fresh cilantro, for garnish (optional)

## STEPS

1. Preheat the air fryer to 325°F. Toast coriander and cumin seeds in a dry pan for about 50-60 seconds over medium heat until fragrant. Grind finely using a mortar and pestle or spice grinder.
2. Toss the carrots in a bowl with coconut oil, minced garlic, toasted spice mixture, salt, and pepper.
3. Place the seasoned carrots on a greased plate in the air fryer basket. Cook for 12-15 minutes, stirring occasionally, until crispy and golden brown.
4. Garnish with fresh cilantro if desired.

## NUTRITIONAL SERVING

Protein: 1g, Carb: 12g, Fat: 4g, Sodium: 2g, Sugar: 2g, Potassium: 3g, Calories: Approx. 80-100 kcal per serving.

## Recipe Tips:

For an extra flavor kick, sprinkle a small amount of chili powder over the carrots before air frying.

## 12.8 Easy Garlic Knots

Easy Garlic Knots are a delightful twist on traditional garlic bread. Made with whole wheat flour and Greek yogurt, these knots are not only tasty but also a healthier option. They're perfect as a side or snack, especially with their aromatic garlic and parmesan topping.

**PREPARATION TIME:** 30 minutes
**Cooking Time:** 20 minutes
**DIFFICULTY LEVEL:** Hard
**SERVINGS:** 2

### INGREDIENTS

- Olive oil spray
- Whole wheat white flour, 1 cup
- Salt, ¾ tsp
- Baking powder, 2 tbsp
- Greek yogurt, 1 cup
- Butter, 2 tbsp
- Garlic cloves, 3, minced
- Grated Parmesan cheese, 1 tbsp
- Chopped parsley, 1 tbsp

### STEPS

1. Preheat your oven to 450°F. Line a baking sheet with a silicone baking mat or parchment paper.
2. In a large bowl, mix together the flour, salt, and baking powder. Stir in the Greek yogurt until a dough forms. If the dough is sticky, add a bit more flour. Knead the dough about 15 times with dry hands.
3. Divide the dough into 8 equal pieces. Roll each piece into a 9-inch long rope.
4. Tie each rope into a knot and place on the prepared baking sheet.
5. Bake in the upper third of the oven for about 20 minutes, or until golden brown. Let cool for 5 minutes.
6. In a skillet, melt butter and sauté the garlic for 2 minutes until golden.
7. Toss the garlic knots in the garlic butter, or brush them using a pastry brush. If they seem dry, add an extra spritz of olive oil.
8. Sprinkle with parsley and Parmesan cheese before serving.

### NUTRITIONAL SERVING

Protein: 15g, Carb: 16g, Fat: 10g, Sodium: 2g, Sugar: 2g, Potassium: 3g, Calories: Approx. 180-200 kcal per serving.

### Recipe Tips:

To keep the knots soft, cover them with a clean cloth after they come out of the oven until ready to serve.

## 12.9 Roasted Green Beans

Roasted Green Beans are a delicious and healthy side dish, offering a perfect balance of flavors with a touch of Italian seasoning. This recipe brings out the natural sweetness of green beans and mushrooms, making it an excellent accompaniment to any main course

**PREPARATION TIME:** 40 minutes
**Cooking Time:** 20-24 minutes
**DIFFICULTY LEVEL:** Hard
**SERVINGS:** 2

### INGREDIENTS

- Fresh green beans, 1 lb
- Mushrooms, ½ lb
- Onion, finely chopped, 1 small
- Olive oil, 2 tsp
- Italian seasoning, 1 tsp
- Salt, ¼ tsp

- Mustard, 1/8 tsp

## STEPS

1. Preheat the air fryer to 375°F.
2. In a large mixing bowl, combine green beans, mushrooms, onion, olive oil, Italian seasoning, salt, and mustard. Toss well to evenly coat the vegetables.
3. Place the seasoned vegetables on an oiled tray in the air fryer basket.
4. Cook for 10-12 minutes, stirring occasionally, until the vegetables start to soften. For extra crispiness, flip and cook for an additional 10-12 minutes or until golden brown.

## NUTRITIONAL SERVING

Protein: 1g, Carb: 6g, Fat: 3g, Sodium: 2g, Sugar: 2g, Potassium: 3g, Calories: Approx. 60-70 kcal per serving.

## Recipe Tips:

For a variation, try adding a splash of balsamic vinegar before the final stage of cooking for a tangy twist.

# Chapter 12: Substitute Ingredients Guide

## 12.1 Veggie Chip Medley:
Vegetarian:
- Already vegetarian-friendly.

Gluten-Free:
- Recipe is naturally gluten-free.

Allergen-Free:
- Replace olive oil with another preferred cooking oil for those with olive allergies.

## 12.2 Twice Air Fried Vegan Stuffed Idaho Potatoes:
Vegetarian:
- Already vegetarian-friendly.

Gluten-Free:
- Recipe is naturally gluten-free.

Allergen-Free:
- Replace olive oil with another preferred cooking oil for those with olive allergies.

## 12.3 Potato Chips:
Vegetarian:
- Already vegetarian-friendly.

Gluten-Free:
- Recipe is naturally gluten-free.

Allergen-Free:
- Replace olive oil spray with another cooking spray suitable for those with olive allergies.

## 12.4 Radishes:
Vegetarian:
- Already vegetarian-friendly.

Gluten-Free:
- Recipe is naturally gluten-free.

Allergen-Free:
- Replace olive oil with another preferred cooking oil for those with olive allergies.

## 12.5 General Tso's Cauliflower:
Vegetarian:
- Already vegetarian-friendly.

Gluten-Free:
- Replace flour with a gluten-free flour variant.

Allergen-Free:
- Replace flour with a non-allergenic flour substitute like rice flour.

## 12.6 Green Tomato Stacks:
Vegetarian:
- Replace Canadian bacon slices with vegetarian bacon or another protein substitute like tofu slices.

Gluten-Free:
- Replace flour with a gluten-free variant.
- Replace cornmeal with gluten-free cornmeal or almond meal.

Allergen-Free:
- Replace mayonnaise with egg-free mayonnaise for those allergic to eggs.

## 12.7 Cumin Carrots:
Vegetarian:
- Already vegetarian-friendly.

Gluten-Free:
- Recipe is naturally gluten-free.

Allergen-Free:
- If coconut oil allergy is a concern, substitute with another preferred cooking oil.

## 12.8 Easy Garlic Knots:
Vegetarian:
- Already vegetarian-friendly.

Gluten-Free:
- Replace whole wheat flour white with a gluten-free flour blend.

Allergen-Free:
- Ensure that the Greek yogurt used is free from potential allergens.
- Replace butter with a non-dairy alternative for those with dairy allergies.

## 12.9 Roasted Green Beans
**Vegetarian:** No changes needed as the recipe is already vegetarian.

**Gluten-Free:** The recipe is already gluten-free, but always ensure any store-bought ingredients like mustard are certified gluten-free if sensitivity is high.

**Allergen-Free:** (Note: Always refer to allergens that are commonly known, like dairy, nuts, soy, etc. The exact allergens to be avoided would depend on individual needs.)
- Mustard, 1/8 tsp: Some mustards may contain additives or preservatives that could be allergenic for some individuals. Always read the label and consider using homemade mustard or omitting if necessary.

Always advise readers to check labels on store-bought products to ensure they meet individual dietary needs. Also, this guide addresses common vegetarian, gluten-free, and general allergen replacements. Personal allergies and sensitivities can vary, and not all replacements may be suitable for everyone. Always consult with a healthcare provider if unsure.

# Chapter 13: Dessert Recipes

## 13.1 Lemon Butterfly Buns

Lemon Butterfly Buns are a delightful and visually charming treat, perfect for an afternoon snack or a sweet addition to any gathering. These buns are light, fluffy, and have a zesty lemon flavor that's irresistible.

**PREPARATION TIME:** 20 minutes
**Cooking Time:** 8 minutes per batch
**DIFFICULTY LEVEL:** Medium
**SERVINGS:** 2

**INGREDIENTS**
- Butter, ½ cup
- Sugar, ½ cup
- 2 medium Eggs
- Flour, ½ cup
- Vanilla essence, ½ tsp.
- Icing sugar, ½ cup
- Small lemon, juiced
- Cherries for decoration

**STEPS**
1. Preheat the air fryer to 170°C.
2. In a large bowl, cream together butter and sugar until light and fluffy.
3. Stir in vanilla essence.
4. Gradually add eggs, ensuring each addition is well incorporated. Add a little flour to prevent curdling.
5. Sift in the remaining flour and fold gently into the mixture.
6. Spoon half of the mixture into mini bun cases until you run out of cases. Bake the first six buns for 8 minutes at 170°C in the air fryer.
7. While buns are baking, prepare the icing. Cream the butter and gradually add icing sugar. Mix in lemon juice until completely smooth. Add a little water if the mixture is too thick.
8. Cut the top off each baked bun, slice them in half to form butterfly wings. Spread some icing in the center of the bun, place a cherry in the middle, and lightly dust the top of the cherry with icing sugar.
9. Serve and enjoy the lemony delight.

**NUTRITIONAL SERVING**
- Protein: 4g, Carbs: 60g, Fat: 25g, Sodium: 150mg, Sugar: 35g , Calories: ~450 kcal

**Recipe Tips:** For an extra lemony flavor, add lemon zest to the batter.

## 13.2 Apple Crisp

Apple Crisp is a classic dessert that combines the sweet and tangy flavors of apples with a crispy, crumbly topping. It's a comforting and delightful treat, perfect for any occasion.

**PREPARATION TIME:** 30 minutes
**Cooking Time:** 13 minutes
**DIFFICULTY LEVEL:** Hard
**SERVINGS:** 2

**INGREDIENTS**
- 6 medium Apples, peeled and chopped
- 1 tbsp. Sugar
- 1 tbsp. Cinnamon
- ½ cup Flour
- ½ cup Sugar
- ½ cup Butter
- ½ cup Oats

## STEPS

1. Place the chopped apples in a mixing bowl.
2. Mix 1 tbsp. sugar and cinnamon in a bowl and sprinkle over the apples. Transfer to ramekins.
3. In a separate bowl, combine butter and flour, mixing until it forms coarse breadcrumbs.
4. Stir in ½ cup sugar and oats into the breadcrumb mixture.
5. Cover the apples in the ramekins with the oat mixture.
6. Cook in the air fryer at 160 °C (320 °F) for 8 minutes, then increase the temperature to 200 °C (400 °F) and cook for an additional 5 minutes.

### NUTRITIONAL SERVING:

Protein: 2g, Carbs: 60g, Fat: 20g, Sodium: 200mg, Sugar: 45g, Calories: ~450 kcal

**Recipe Tips:** For a crisper topping, add a handful of chopped nuts to the oat mixture.

## 13.3 Chocolate Mug Cake

Chocolate Mug Cake offers a quick and indulgent treat, perfect for satisfying your sweet tooth. It's a simple yet delicious dessert that you can whip up in no time, making it ideal for last-minute cravings.

**PREPARATION TIME:** 20 minutes
**Cooking Time:** 10 minutes
**DIFFICULTY LEVEL:** Medium

**SERVINGS:** 2

### INGREDIENTS

24. Flour, ¼ cup
25. Sugar, 5 tbsp.
26. Cocoa powder, 1 tbsp.
27. Milk, 3 tbsp.
28. Coconut oil, 3 tsp.

## STEPS

1. Thoroughly mix all ingredients in a mug, ensuring they are well combined to avoid uneven chocolate distribution.
2. Refrigerate the mixture for 10 minutes.
3. Bake in the air fryer at 200°C for 10 minutes.
4. Repeat the process with any remaining cups.

### NUTRITIONAL SERVING

- Protein: 4g, Carbs: 60g, Fat: 12g, Sodium: 50mg, Sugar: 40g, Calories: ~300 kcal

**Recipe Tips:** For a molten center, reduce the cooking time slightly, allowing the middle to remain gooey.

## 13.4 Blueberry Jam Tarts

Blueberry Jam Tarts are a delightful treat, combining the sweetness of blueberry jam with a crisp, buttery pastry. These tarts are a perfect choice for tea time or as a dessert.

**PREPARATION TIME:** 20 minutes
**Cooking Time:** 10 minutes
**DIFFICULTY LEVEL:** Hard
**SERVINGS:** 2

### INGREDIENTS

29. Pie crust, 2 cups
30. Blueberry Jam, 3 cups

### STEPS

1. Flour the tart tins to prevent the crust from sticking.
2. Roll out the pie crust on a surface and place it in the tart pans.
3. Generously fill each tart with blueberry jam.
4. Air fry in an oven pan for 10 minutes at 180°C/360°F.
5. Serve warm or cool.

### NUTRITIONAL SERVING

Protein: 3g, Carbs: 75g, Fat: 22g, Sodium: 150mg, Sugar: 40g, Calories: ~500 kcal

**Recipe Tips:** For a golden-brown finish, lightly brush the crust with an egg wash before baking.

## 13.5 Chocolate Orange Fondant

Chocolate Orange Fondant is a rich, indulgent dessert featuring a molten chocolate center with a hint of zesty orange. It's an elegant choice for a special occasion or a cozy night in.

**PREPARATION TIME:** 20 minutes
**Cooking Time:** 13 minutes
**DIFFICULTY LEVEL:** Hard
**SERVINGS:** 2
**INGREDIENTS**
- 2 tbsp. Flour
- 4 tbsp. Sugar
- ½ cup Dark chocolate
- ½ cup Butter
- 1 medium Orange
- 2 medium Eggs

**STEPS**
1. Preheat the air fryer to 180°C.
2. Melt the butter and chocolate in a bowl over a pot of boiling water. Stir until smooth.
3. Whisk the eggs and sugar until light and frothy.
4. Fold the chocolate mixture into the egg mixture. Stir in the grated zest of the orange. Gently fold in the flour.
5. Pour the batter into greased ramekins, filling them up. Air fry for approximately 11 minutes.
6. Let the fondants rest for a minute, then carefully invert onto plates.

**NUTRITIONAL SERVING**
Protein: 6g, Carbs: 60g, Fat: 35g, Sodium: 200mg, Sugar: 50g, Calories: ~550 kcal

**Recipe Tips:** Serve the fondant right after cooking for the best molten center.

## 13.6 Pumpkin Pie

Pumpkin Pie is a classic dessert that combines the earthy sweetness of pumpkin with warm spices, encased in a flaky crust. It's a comforting treat, perfect for any autumn gathering or as a cozy winter dessert.

**PREPARATION TIME:** 30 minutes
**Cooking Time:** 24 minutes
**DIFFICULTY LEVEL:** Hard
**SERVINGS:** 2
**INGREDIENTS**
- 1 cup Flour
- ½ cup Butter
- 3 tbsp. Sugar
- 1 tbsp. Cinnamon
- 1 tsp. Nutmeg
- 1 cup Pumpkin puree
- 1 Egg
- ¼ cup Milk

**STEPS**
1. Make the pie crust by combining flour and butter until it resembles breadcrumbs. Add a little water to form a dough. Press the dough into a pie pan.
2. In another bowl, mix pumpkin puree, sugar, cinnamon, nutmeg, egg, and milk until smooth.
3. Pour the pumpkin mixture into the pie crust.
4. Preheat the air fryer to 180°C and bake the pie for 24 minutes, or until the filling is set and the crust is golden.
5. Let the pie cool before serving. Refrigerate for better consistency.

**NUTRITIONAL SERVING**
Protein: 6g, Carbs: 50g, Fat: 15g, Sodium: 200mg,

Sugar: 20g, Calories: ~350 kcal

**Recipe Tips:** Chill the pie before serving to allow the filling to set properly.

## 13.7 Leftover Coconut Sugar Recipes

This unique recipe transforms leftover ingredients, particularly coconut sugar, into a delightful dessert. It's a creative way to use up pantry items, resulting in a delicious treat that's both sweet and satisfying.

**PREPARATION TIME:** 25 minutes
**Cooking Time:** 15 minutes
**DIFFICULTY LEVEL:** Medium
**SERVINGS:** 2

**INGREDIENTS**
- 3 cups Flour
- 2 cups Butter
- ½ cup Cheese
- 1 cup Coconut sugar
- 2 tbsp. Honey
- 1 tsp. Vanilla essence
- 1 tsp. Cinnamon

**STEPS**
1. Preheat the air fryer to 180 degrees Celsius.
2. In a bowl, mix flour, butter, and coconut sugar until it resembles breadcrumbs.
3. Stir in cinnamon and honey until the dough starts to come together.
4. Divide the dough: 2/5 for the base, 1/5 for later use, and the remaining 2/5 for the top layer.
5. Line the air fryer with a baking mat.
6. Form a thin layer of dough in the air fryer as the base.
7. Bake for 5 minutes at 180°C.
8. While the base is chilling, prepare the filling by mixing cheese with 2/5 of the dough to form a cheesecake-like consistency. Add the blackberries on top of the crust in the air fryer.
9. Crumble the remaining dough over the top.
10. Bake for 15 minutes at 180°C until a nice crumble forms.
11. Chill in the fridge to set before slicing into bars.

**NUTRITIONAL SERVING**

Protein: 5g, Carbs: 31g, Fat: 20g, Sodium: 200mg, Sugar: 20g, Calories: ~450 kcal

.

**Recipe Tips:** Ensure the dough for the base is thin for optimal texture.

## 13.8 Mince Pies

Mince pies are a classic holiday treat, filled with rich, spiced mincemeat in a flaky, buttery crust. These pies are a festive delight, perfect for enjoying during the winter season.

**PREPARATION TIME:** 30 minutes
**Cooking Time:** 15 minutes
**DIFFICULTY LEVEL:** Medium
**SERVINGS:** 2

**INGREDIENTS**
- 3 cups Pie crust
- 2 cups Jar mincemeat
- 1 small Egg
- ¼ cup Icing sugar
- Flour for dusting

**STEPS**
1. In a bowl, combine the ingredients for the pie crust. Work the butter into the flour until it resembles breadcrumbs, then mix in the sugar. Gradually add water and blend to form a smooth dough. Roll out the dough and fit it into pie pans.
2. Fill each pie with mincemeat, but avoid overfilling.
3. Use a pastry cutter to cut the dough to the appropriate size for covering the pies. Place the dough tops over the mincemeat, pressing down gently.
4. Before placing the pies in the air fryer, brush their tops with beaten egg. Air fry at 180°C/360°F for 15 minutes.
5. Serve immediately or store for later. Sprinkle with icing sugar for a finishing touch.

**NUTRITIONAL SERVING**

Protein: 4g, Carbs: 21g, Fat: 20g, Sodium: 200mg, Sugar: 20g, Calories: ~300 kcal

**Recipe Tips:** For a festive twist, add a splash of brandy or rum to the mincemeat filling.

## 13.9 Brownies

Indulge in these rich, fudgy brownies, featuring a deep chocolate flavor with a hint of vanilla. Perfect for satisfying any chocolate craving, these brownies are a classic treat for any occasion.

**PREPARATION TIME:** 25 minutes
**DIFFICULTY LEVEL:** Medium
**SERVINGS:** 2

**INGREDIENTS**
31. Flour, ½ cup
32. Butter, ½ cup
33. Eggs, 2 large
34. Cocoa powder, 3 tbsp
35. Brown sugar, 2 cups
36. Golden syrup, 1 tbsp.
37. Vanilla essence, 2 tsp.

**STEPS**
1. Preheat your air fryer to the recommended temperature for baking.
2. In a mixing bowl, cream together the butter and brown sugar until light and fluffy.
3. Beat in the eggs one at a time, followed by the vanilla essence and golden syrup.
4. Sift in the flour and cocoa powder, gently folding into the wet ingredients until just combined.
5. Pour the batter into a suitable air fryer-safe baking dish or pan.

6. Bake in the air fryer until a toothpick inserted into the center comes out mostly clean with a few moist crumbs (time may vary based on your air fryer model).
7. Allow to cool before cutting into squares and serving.

**NUTRITIONAL SERVING**

Protein: 11g, Carbs: 97g, Fat: 11g, Sodium: 200mg, Sugar: 97g, Calories: ~800 kcal

**Recipe Tips:** For extra richness, add chocolate chips or nuts to the batter before baking.

## 13.10 Chocolate Eclairs in The Air Fryer

Experience the delight of homemade chocolate eclairs made effortlessly in your air fryer. These delicate pastries are filled with a rich cream and topped with a smooth chocolate glaze, offering a perfect balance of sweetness and texture.

**PREPARATION TIME:** 15 minutes
**Cooking Time:** 18 minutes
**DIFFICULTY LEVEL:** Medium
**SERVINGS:** 2

**INGREDIENTS**
38. Butter, ¼ cup
39. Flour, ½ cup
40. Medium eggs, 3
41. Water, 150 ml

**STEPS**
1. Preheat your air fryer to 180°C (356°F).
2. In a large saucepan, melt the butter over medium heat and bring to a boil with the water.
3. Remove from heat and gradually stir in the flour, returning to the heat and stirring continuously until a smooth dough forms.

4. Transfer the dough to a mixing bowl and let it cool slightly. Gradually add the eggs, mixing until you have a smooth, glossy dough.
5. Pipe the dough into éclair shapes on a baking tray suitable for your air fryer.
6. Bake the eclairs in the air fryer for 10 minutes at 180°C, then lower the temperature to 160°C (320°F) and continue baking for another 8 minutes.
7. For the cream filling, whisk together heavy cream, vanilla extract, and icing sugar until thick and smooth.
8. Once the eclairs are baked, let them cool before filling them with the cream and topping with a chocolate glaze.

**NUTRITIONAL SERVING**
Protein: 10g, Carbs: 12g, Fat: 9g, Sodium: 200mg, Sugar: 5g, Calories: ~200 kcal

**Recipe Tips:** For a glossy finish on your eclairs, brush them with egg wash before baking.

## 13.11 Chocolate Profiteroles

Indulge in the classic French dessert, Chocolate Profiteroles, right from your kitchen. These airy choux pastries filled with sweet cream and topped with a rich chocolate glaze are a delightful treat that combines the elegance of French patisserie with the convenience of your air fryer.

**PREPARATION TIME:** 10 minutes
**Cooking Time:** 18 minutes
**DIFFICULTY LEVEL:** Easy
**SERVINGS:** 2
**INGREDIENTS**
- Butter, ½ cup
- Flour, 1 cup
- Eggs, 6 medium
- Water, ¼ cup

**STEPS**

1. Set your air fryer to 170°C (338°F).
2. In a large saucepan, combine butter and water. Bring to a boil over medium heat.
3. Remove from heat, quickly stir in the flour, then return to heat and stir until a smooth dough forms.
4. Transfer the dough to a mixing bowl and cool slightly. Gradually add eggs, mixing until you have a smooth, glossy dough.
5. Form the dough into small balls or profiterole shapes. Bake in the air fryer for 8-10 minutes at 180°C (356°F).
6. For the cream filling, mix whipped cream, vanilla extract, and icing sugar until thick and smooth.
7. Prepare the chocolate glaze by melting chocolate, cream, and butter in a bowl set over simmering water. Stir until smooth.
8. Once profiteroles are cooked and cooled, fill them with cream and drizzle with the chocolate glaze.

**NUTRITIONAL SERVING**
Protein: 17g, Carbs: 45g, Fat: 13g, Sodium: 200mg, Sugar: 10g, Calories: ~350 kcal

**Recipe Tips:** For perfectly risen profiteroles, avoid opening the air fryer frequently during baking.

## 13.12 Doughnuts from Scratch

Homemade doughnuts bring a warm, comforting treat to your table. These light, fluffy delights, easily made in an air fryer, provide the perfect canvas for a variety of sweet toppings. Enjoy the classic taste of freshly made doughnuts without the hassle of deep frying.

**PREPARATION TIME:** 20 minutes
**Cooking Time:** 8 minute
**DIFFICULTY LEVEL:** Medium
**SERVINGS:** 2

**INGREDIENTS**
42. Doughnut dough, 3 cups
43. Icing sugar, 1 cup

44. Milk, ¼ cup
45. Vanilla essence, 1 tsp.
46. Extra virgin olive oil spray
47. Flour for dusting
48. Food coloring (optional)

### STEPS

1. On a floured surface, roll out the doughnut dough. Use additional flour as needed to prevent sticking.
2. Use biscuit cutters to cut out large doughnut shapes and a smaller cutter for the holes. Set aside the doughnut holes.
3. Cook up to 4 doughnuts at a time in the air fryer basket at 180°C (356°F) for 8 minutes. Halfway through, spray with olive oil for a golden finish.
4. In a bowl, mix milk and icing sugar to create a thick glaze. Divide into separate ramekins and add food coloring for various colors. Dip the doughnuts into the glaze and top with sprinkles.
5. Serve the doughnuts fresh and enjoy.

### NUTRITIONAL SERVING

Protein: 5g, Carb: 15g, Fat: 11g, Sodium: 2g, Sugar: 2g, Potassium: 3g.

## 13.13 Churros

These homemade Churros offer a delightful combination of a crispy exterior and a soft interior, with a sweet and spiced flavor from the cinnamon-sugar coating. A classic treat in many cultures, these Churros are perfect for satisfying a sweet tooth.

**Preparation time: 10** minutes
Cooking Time: 5 minutes
**Difficulty Level:** Easy
**Servings:** 2

### Ingredients

- Butter, 1/4 cup
- A pinch of salt
- Milk, 1/2 cup
- Eggs, 2
- All-purpose flour, 1/2 cup
- Ground cinnamon, 1/2 tsp
- Granulated white sugar, 1/4 cup

### Steps

1. In a saucepan, combine butter, salt, and milk. Bring to a simmer over medium heat, stirring occasionally.
2. Once simmering, reduce heat to low and add the flour, stirring continuously until a batter forms.
3. Remove the pan from the heat and let it cool for about 5 minutes. Then, beat in the eggs until well combined.
4. Fill a piping bag fitted with a star tip with the batter. Pipe the dough into 4-6 inch long strips directly into the preheated air fryer basket.
5. Air fry the churros at 340°F for approximately 5 minutes or until they are golden brown.
6. In the meantime, mix the cinnamon and sugar in a shallow dish.
7. Once the churros are cooked, roll them in the cinnamon-sugar mixture until well coated.

### Nutritional Serving

Protein: 6g, Carbs: 36g, Fat: 15g, Sodium: 100mg, Sugar: 12g, Fiber: 1g.

**Recipe Tips:** For the best texture, pipe the churros dough while it's still warm, and ensure your air fryer is preheated for even cooking.

## 13.14 Butter Cake

Savor the simple yet irresistible charm of a classic Butter Cake. Its rich, buttery flavor and moist texture make it a timeless treat for any occasion.

**PREPARATION TIME:** 10 minutes

**DIFFICULTY LEVEL:** Easy
**SERVINGS:** 2

**INGREDIENTS**
- 7 tbsp Butter
- Cooking spray
- ¼ Cup Sugar
- 2 tbsp White Sugar
- 1 Large Egg
- 2/3 Cup Flour
- 6 tbsp Milk
- A pinch of Salt

**STEPS**
1. Preheat the air fryer to 350°F. Use cooking spray to grease a small, fluted tube pan.
2. In a bowl, use an electric mixer to cream together the butter and 1/4 cup plus 2 tbsp of sugar until light and fluffy. Add the egg and beat until smooth.
3. In a separate bowl, mix flour and salt. Gradually add this to the creamed mixture, alternating with milk, until fully incorporated. Pour the batter into the prepared pan, leveling the top with a wooden spoon.
4. Place the pan in the air fryer basket and set to cook for 15 minutes, or until a toothpick inserted into the center of the cake comes out clean.
5. Remove the cake from the pan and let it cool for about 5 minutes.

**NUTRITIONAL SERVING**
Protein: 8g, Carbs: 60g, Fat: 30g, Sodium: 200mg, Sugar: 30g, Calories: ~520 kcal.

**Recipe Tips:** Serve the cake warm for a softer and riche

## 13.15 Chocolate Cake

This simple yet delightful chocolate cake is a perfect treat for any occasion. Its rich flavor and moist texture make it a favorite among chocolate lovers.

**PREPARATION TIME:** 15 minutes
**Cooking Time:** 15 minutes
**DIFFICULTY LEVEL:** Medium
**SERVINGS:** 2

**INGREDIENTS**
- ¼ Cup White Sugar
- 3 ½ tbsp. Butter
- 1 Large Egg
- Cooking Spray
- 1 tbsp. Apricot Jam
- 1 tbsp. Flour
- 1 tbsp. Cocoa Powder
- A Pinch of Salt

**STEPS**
1. Preheat the air fryer to 320°F (160°C). Coat a small, fluted tube pan with cooking spray.
2. In a bowl, use an electric mixer to blend the butter and sugar until foamy. Mix in the apricot jam and egg until smooth. Then add the flour, cocoa powder, and a pinch of salt, blending thoroughly.
3. Pour the batter into the prepared pan, leveling the top with a spoon.
4. Place the pan in the air fryer basket. Cook for 15 minutes, or until a toothpick inserted into the center of the cake comes out clean.
5. Allow the cake to cool in the pan for about five minutes before transferring to a wire rack to cool completely.

**NUTRITIONAL SERVING**
Protein: 7g, Carbs: 60g, Fat: 28g, Sodium: 400mg, Sugar: 40g, Calories: ~520 kcal.

**Recipe Tips:** For an extra indulgent treat, serve the cake with a scoop of vanilla ice cream or a drizzle of chocolate sauce.

## 13.16 Cannoli

Indulge in the classic Italian treat of Cannoli, transformed for the air fryer. These crispy, sweet, and creamy delights, filled with ricotta and chocolate chips, offer a taste of Italy in every bite.

**PREPARATION TIME:** 15 minutes
**Cooking Time:** 12-13 minutes
**DIFFICULTY LEVEL:** Medium
**SERVINGS:** 2

### INGREDIENTS
49. 1 Package Milk Ricotta, strained
50. ½ Cup Powdered Sugar
51. 1 Tbsp. Orange Zest
52. ½ Tsp. Salt
53. 1 Cup Turbinado Sugar
54. 1 Package Pre-made Pie Crusts
55. 1 Large Egg White
56. ½ Cup Chocolate Chips
57. ½ Cup Roasted Pistachios, crushed

### STEPS
1. Strain ricotta through a cheesecloth-lined strainer to remove excess liquid. In a medium bowl, whisk together the strained ricotta, orange zest, salt, and powdered sugar. Transfer the mixture into a piping bag.
2. Roll out pie crusts to 1/16-inch thickness on a floured surface. Cut out 16 rectangles (3 1/2 inches each). Wrap each around a cannoli mold, sealing the edges with egg white. Lightly brush the entire surface with egg white and roll in turbinado sugar.
3. Lightly coat the air fryer basket with cooking spray. Place the cannoli, spaced about 3/4 inch apart, in the basket. Air fry at 400°F for 5-7 minutes or until golden and crisp. Remove with tongs, cool for a minute, then gently slide off the molds. Let cool for 10 minutes. Repeat with remaining shells.

4. Pipe the ricotta mixture into the cooled cannoli shells. Dip each end in chocolate chips or crushed pistachios. Dust with powdered sugar before serving.

**NUTRITIONAL SERVING**
Protein: 9g, Carbs: 55g, Fat: 20g, Sodium: 250mg, Sugar: 30g, Calories: ~450 kcal

**Recipe Tips:** For an extra flavor boost, add a hint of vanilla or almond extract to the ricotta mixture.

## 13.17 Baked Apples

Savor the sweet and warm goodness of these air fryer baked apples. Filled with a delicious mix of oats and spices, they offer a comforting and healthy dessert option.

**PREPARATION TIME:** 15 minutes
Cooking Time: 9 minutes
**DIFFICULTY LEVEL:** Easy
**SERVINGS:** 2

### INGREDIENTS
- Apples, 2 (cored)
- Raisins, 2 tbsp.
- Oats, ¼ cup
- Walnuts, chopped, 2 tbsp.
- Cinnamon, ½ tsp.
- Brown sugar, 1 tbsp.
- Butter, 1 tsp. (melted)

### STEPS
1. Preheat your air fryer to 350°F.
2. In a bowl, combine the raisins, oats, chopped walnuts, cinnamon, and brown sugar. Melt the butter and mix it in until all the ingredients are well combined. Set aside.
3. Slice off the top and bottom of each apple. Use a paring knife or an apple corer to remove the core and seeds.

4. Stuff each apple with the cinnamon oat mixture. Place the stuffed apples in the air fryer basket.

5. Cook for about 9 minutes or until the apples are soft to your liking. Let the apples cool before serving.

## NUTRITIONAL SERVING

Protein: 36g, Carb: 5g, Fat: 0g, Sodium: 2g, Sugar: 2g, Potassium: 3g.

**Recipe Tips:** For a nut-free option, you can replace walnuts with pumpkin seeds or simply omit them.

# Chapter 13: Substitute Ingredients Guide

## 13.1 Lemon Butterfly Buns:
Vegetarian:
- Replace Butter with Vegan Butter or Margarine **Gluten-Free:**
- Replace Flour with Gluten-free Flour **Allergen-Free:**
- Replace Eggs with Flaxseed eggs (1 tbsp ground flaxseed + 2.5 tbsp water per egg) or a commercial egg replacement

## 13.2 Apple Crisp:
Vegetarian:
- Replace Butter with Vegan Butter or Margarine **Gluten-Free:**
- Replace Flour with Gluten-free Flour or Almond Flour
- Oats with Certified Gluten-free Oats **Allergen-Free:** No major allergens identified.

## 13.3 Chocolate Mug Cake:
Vegetarian: No modifications needed.
Gluten-Free:
- Replace Flour with Gluten-free Flour

Allergen-Free:
- Replace Milk with a non-dairy milk like Almond or Soy Milk.

## 13.4 Blueberry Jam Tarts:
Vegetarian: No modifications needed.
Gluten-Free:
- Replace Pie Crust with a Gluten-free Pie Crust **Allergen-Free:** Ensure the Blueberry Jam is free from any allergens.

## 13.5 Chocolate Orange Fondant:
Vegetarian:
- Replace Butter with Vegan Butter or Margarine **Gluten-Free:**
- Replace Flour with Gluten-free Flour **Allergen-Free:**
- Replace Eggs with Flaxseed eggs (1 tbsp ground flaxseed + 2.5 tbsp water per egg) or a commercial egg replacement

## 13.6 Pumpkin Pie:
Vegetarian:
- Replace Butter with Vegan Butter or Margarine **Gluten-Free:**
- Replace Flour with Gluten-free Flour or Almond Flour **Allergen-Free:** No major allergens identified.

## 13.7 Leftover Coconut Sugar Recipes:
Vegetarian:
- Replace Butter with Vegan Butter or Margarine **Gluten-Free:**
- Replace Flour with Gluten-free Flour **Allergen-Free:**
- Ensure Cheese is lactose-free or replace with a lactose-free cheese alternative

## 13.8 Mince Pies:
Vegetarian: No modifications needed. Gluten-Free:
- Replace Pie Crust with a Gluten-free Pie Crust
- Ensure Jar Mincemeat is gluten-free **Allergen-Free:**
- Replace Egg with a commercial egg replacement or brush with non-dairy milk

## 13.9 Brownies:
Vegetarian:
- Replace Butter with Vegan Butter or Margarine **Gluten-Free:**
- Replace Flour with Gluten-free Flour or Almond Flour **Allergen-Free:**
- Replace Eggs with Flaxseed eggs (1 tbsp ground flaxseed + 2.5 tbsp water per egg) or a commercial egg replacement

## 13.10 Chocolate Eclairs in The Air Fryer:
Vegetarian:
- Butter: Substitute with plant-based butter or margarine.

Gluten-Free:
- Flour: Substitute with gluten-free all-purpose flour. Make sure to adjust the consistency if needed, as gluten-free flour can behave differently.

Allergen-Free:
- Butter: Substitute with allergen-free margarine or coconut oil.
- Eggs: Substitute 3 medium eggs with a combination of 9 tablespoons of water and 3 tablespoons of ground flaxseeds (let sit for 10 minutes to thicken).
- Flour: Substitute with allergen-free all-purpose flour or rice flour.

## 13.11 Chocolate Profiteroles:
Vegetarian:
- Butter: Substitute with plant-based butter or margarine.

Gluten-Free:

- Flour: Substitute with gluten-free all-purpose flour. Adjust consistency if needed.

Allergen-Free:

- Butter: Substitute with allergen-free margarine or coconut oil.
- Eggs: Substitute 6 medium eggs with a combination of 12 tablespoons of water and 6 tablespoons of ground flaxseeds (let sit for 10 minutes to thicken).
- Flour: Substitute with allergen-free all-purpose flour or rice flour.

## 13.12 Doughnuts from Scratch:

Vegetarian:

- No substitutions needed.

Gluten-Free:

- Doughnut dough: Use gluten-free doughnut dough.
- Flour: Substitute with gluten-free all-purpose flour. Adjust consistency if needed.

Allergen-Free:

- Doughnut dough: Make sure to use allergen-free doughnut dough.
- Milk: Substitute with allergen-free milk alternatives like almond, rice, or oat milk.
- Flour: Substitute with allergen-free all-purpose flour or rice flour.
- Extra virgin olive oil spray: Check labels to ensure it's allergen-free, or use coconut oil spray.

## 13.13 Churros

- **Vegan**: Substitute "Eggs" with a vegan egg replacer, "Butter" with vegan butter, and "Milk" with almond or oat milk.
- **Gluten-Free**: Replace "All-purpose flour" with "Gluten-free flour".
- **Allergen-Free**: Use almond milk or oat milk and vegan substitutes for eggs and butter.

## 13.14 Butter Cake:

Vegetarian:

- No substitutions needed.

Gluten-Free:

- Flour: Use gluten-free flour.

Allergen-Free:

- Butter: Use allergen-free or dairy-free butter.

## 13.15 Chocolate Cake:

Vegetarian:

- No substitutions needed.

Gluten-Free:

- Flour: Use gluten-free flour.

Allergen-Free:

- Butter: Use allergen-free or dairy-free butter.

## 13.16 Cannoli:

Vegetarian:

- No substitutions needed.

Gluten-Free:

- Flour: Use gluten-free flour.
- Freeze piecrusts: Use gluten-free piecrusts.

Allergen-Free:

- Ensure piecrusts are allergen-free.
- Butter: Use dairy-free butter if lactose intolerant.

## 13.17 Baked Apples

58. Vegetarian:

- Already vegetarian.

Gluten-Free:

- Already gluten-free.

Allergen-Free:

- Butter: Use coconut oil or a dairy-free butter substitute.

Note:

- When using gluten-free substitutes, it is important to check the consistency of the batter or dough. Sometimes, you may need to adjust the liquid content or add binding agents like xanthan gum or guar gum to mimic the elasticity provided by gluten.
- For allergen-free substitutions, always check the labels of purchased ingredients to ensure they do not contain traces of allergens.
- The efficacy of egg substitutes can vary depending on the specific recipe. The flaxseed egg replacement tends to work well for baking, but there may be some variation in texture and taste. Adjust accordingly.

# Lend Us Your Voice in Our Journey

As a publisher, every single review is fundamental support for us. Your voice can make a difference and help us continue our mission. If you believe in the value of what we do and want to lend us a hand, please take a moment to share your thoughts. Your review is our beacon in the vast sea of publishing. From the bottom of our hearts, thank you for your invaluable contribution!

Scan the Qr code with the camera of your mobile phone, click on the link that opens and you can leave your review. Thank you.

## https://bit.ly/airfryerkindlerev

# Chapter 14: Snack Recipes

## 14.1 Oreos

A fun twist on classic Oreos, this recipe involves coating the cookies in pancake batter and air frying them for a delightful crispy exterior and soft, chocolatey interior. A treat that's perfect for a quick snack or a special dessert

**PREPARATION TIME:** 10 minutes
**Cooking Time:** 5-6 minutes (plus 2-3 minutes for the second side)
**DIFFICULTY LEVEL:** Medium
**SERVINGS:** 2

**INGREDIENTS**
- ½ cup Pancake mix
- 1/3 cup Water
- Cooking spray
- 9 Chocolate cookies
- 1 tbsp Sugar (powdered)

**STEPS**
1. Blend pancake mix and water in a blender until smooth.
2. Line an air fryer dish with parchment paper. Dip each cookie in the pancake mixture, ensuring they're fully coated.
3. Preheat the air fryer to 400°F. Cook the coated cookies, making sure they do not touch each other. Work in batches if necessary.
4. Cook for 5-6 minutes, then flip and cook for another 2-3 minutes or until slightly browned.
5. Sprinkle powdered sugar on top before serving.

**NUTRITIONAL SERVING**
Protein: 4g, Carbs: 22g, Fat: 12g, Sodium: 200mg, Sugar: 10g , Calories: ~250 kcal

**Recipe Tips:** For a different flavor, try using different types of cookies or adding spices like cinnamon to the pancake batter.

## 14.2 Roasted Bananas

These roasted bananas offer a simple, healthy, and delicious snack. The natural sweetness of the bananas is enhanced through air frying, creating a delightful caramelized treat that's both nutritious and satisfying.

**PREPARATION TIME:** 20 minutes
**Cooking Time:** 5 minutes (plus 2-3 minutes for additional roasting)
**DIFFICULTY LEVEL:** Hard
**SERVINGS:** 2
**INGREDIENTS**
- 1 Banana, sliced into 1/8 inch slices
- Cooking spray (preferably avocado oil)

**STEPS**
1. Preheat the air fryer to 375°F.
2. Arrange banana slices in the basket, ensuring they don't overlap. Work in batches if necessary. Lightly spray the banana slices with avocado oil.
3. Air fry for 5 minutes. Then, carefully flip each slice and continue cooking for an additional 2-3 minutes until the slices are roasted and caramelized.
4. Carefully remove the banana slices from the basket.

**NUTRITIONAL SERVING**
Protein: 1g, Carbs: 27g, Fat: 0g, Sodium: 1mg, Sugar: 14g, Calories: ~110 kcal

**Recipe Tips:** Try sprinkling a little cinnamon or cocoa powder on the banana slices before air frying for an extra flavor kick.

## 14.3 Beignets

Indulge in the light and airy texture of homemade beignets, a classic French pastry. These delightful treats are perfect for satisfying your sweet tooth, bringing a touch of Parisian elegance to your kitchen

**PREPARATION TIME:** 20 minutes
**DIFFICULTY LEVEL:** Medium
**SERVINGS:** 2

**INGREDIENTS**
- ½ Cup Flour
- Cooking spray
- 1/8 Cup Water
- ¼ Cup Sugar
- 1 Large Egg
- ½ tsp Butter
- ½ tsp Baking Powder
- ½ tsp Vanilla Extract
- A pinch of Salt
- 2 tbsp Sugar for dusting

**STEPS**
1. Preheat the air fryer to 365°F (185°C).
2. In a large mixing bowl, combine egg, flour, salt, water, baking powder, sugar, butter, and vanilla extract. Stir to blend the ingredients well.
3. In a small bowl, whip the egg white at medium speed until soft peaks form. Scoop the batter into the prepared mold using a small-hinged ice cream scoop.
4. Place the mold in the air fryer basket.
5. Cook in a preheated air fryer for 10 minutes. Carefully remove the mold from the basket, then release the beignets onto a larger piece of parchment paper.
6. Quickly place the parchment paper with beignets back into the air fryer basket. Cook for an additional 4 minutes. Remove the beignets from the air fryer basket and dust with confectioners' sugar.

**NUTRITIONAL SERVING**
Protein: 5g, Carbs: 60g, Fat: 6g, Sodium: 200mg, Sugar: 24g, Calories: ~330 kcal

**Recipe Tips:** Enjoy these beignets fresh and warm for the best taste and tex

## 14.4 House Gluten-Free Fresh Cherry Crumble

Indulge in the delightful combination of sweet cherries and a buttery crumble in this gluten-free version of a classic cherry crumble. Perfect for a cozy dessert or a special treat

**PREPARATION TIME:** 10 minutes
Cooking Time: 24 minutes
**DIFFICULTY LEVEL:** Easy
**SERVINGS:** 2

**INGREDIENTS**
- 1/3 cup Butter
- 3 cups Cherries
- 10 tbsp White Sugar
- 2 tsp Lemon
- 1 cup Flour (gluten-free)
- 1 tsp Vanilla Powder
- 1 tsp Nutmeg
- 1 tsp Cinnamon

**STEPS**
1. Preheat the air fryer to 165°C (329°F).
2. In a bowl, mix the crushed cherries with 2 tbsp sugar and lemon juice. Stir well and transfer to a baking dish.
3. In a separate bowl, mix the flour with 6 tbsp sugar. Cut the butter into pea-sized pieces and incorporate with the flour until crumbly.
4. Evenly distribute this mixture over the cherries in the baking dish.
5. Combine cinnamon, nutmeg, vanilla powder, and the remaining 2 tbsp sugar in a small bowl. Sprinkle this mixture over the top.

6. Place the dish in the preheated air fryer and cook for about 24 minutes. Check for a golden-brown color; if needed, cook for an additional 5 minutes. Let the dish rest in the air fryer for 10 minutes after turning it off.
7. Remove and let it cool for about 5 minutes before serving.

### NUTRITIONAL SERVING
Protein: 3g, Carbs: 90g, Fat: 18g, Sodium: 300mg, Sugar: 60g, Calories: ~480 kcal

**Recipe Tips:** Serve with a dollop of whipped cream or ice cream for an extra treat.

## 14.5 Double-Glazed Air-Fried Cinnamon Biscuit Bites

Savor the warm, cinnamon-spiced goodness of these Double-Glazed Air-Fried Cinnamon Biscuit Bites. Perfect as a cozy snack or a delightful treat, these bites offer a crispy outside with a soft, flavorful center, topped with a sweet glaze.

**PREPARATION TIME:** 25 minutes
**Cooking Time:** 23-27 minutes
**DIFFICULTY LEVEL:** Hard
**SERVINGS:** 2

### INGREDIENTS
- 2/3 Cup All-Purpose Flour
- 2 Tbsp. Sugar
- 2/3 Cup Whole Wheat Flour
- ¼ Tsp. Cinnamon
- 1 Tsp. Baking Powder
- ¼ Tsp. Salt
- 4 Tbsp. Cold Salted Butter, cubed
- Cooking Spray
- 1/3 Cup Milk
- 3 Tbsp. Water
- 2 Cups Powdered Sugar

### STEPS

1. In a medium bowl, whisk together all-purpose flour, whole wheat flour, sugar, baking powder, cinnamon, and salt. Use a pastry cutter to blend the cold, cubed butter into the flour mixture until it resembles coarse cornmeal. Gradually stir in the milk until the dough forms a cohesive ball.
2. On a floured surface, knead the dough briefly until smooth. Divide the dough into 16 equal pieces and gently roll each piece into a ball.
3. Generously spray the air fryer basket with cooking spray. Place dough balls in the basket, spaced apart, and lightly spray with cooking oil. Air fry at 350°F for 11-12 minutes, or until puffed and golden brown. Carefully remove the doughnut balls to a cooling rack set over foil. Allow cooling for 5 minutes. Repeat with the remaining dough.
4. In a medium bowl, mix powdered sugar and water until smooth. Dip each cooled doughnut ball into the glaze, allowing excess to drip off. Let set for 5 minutes before glazing again.

### NUTRITIONAL SERVING
Protein: 13.5g, Carbs: 100g, Fat: 7g, Sodium: 200mg, Sugar: 50g, Calories: ~600 kcal

**Recipe Tips:** For added crunch and flavor, sprinkle cinnamon sugar over the doughnut bites after the first glaze.

## 14.6 Strawberry "Pop-Tarts"

Enjoy a homemade twist on a classic with these Strawberry "Pop-Tarts." Featuring a flaky crust filled with sweet strawberry jam, these air-fried treats are perfect for a quick snack or a delightful breakfast.

**PREPARATION TIME:** 10 minutes
**Cooking Time:** 10 minutes
**DIFFICULTY LEVEL:** Easy
**SERVINGS:** 2

## INGREDIENTS

- Cooking Spray
- ½ Package Frozen Piecrusts
- ¼ Cup Sugar
- 8 Ounces Strawberries, hulled and chopped
- 1 ½ Tsp. Lemon Juice
- ½ Cup Powdered Sugar
- Candy Sprinkles (optional)

## STEPS

1. In a large microwave-safe bowl, combine strawberries and sugar. Let sit for 15 minutes, stirring occasionally. Microwave on HIGH for 10 minutes, stirring halfway through, until glossy and reduced. Allow cooling for about 30 minutes.
2. On a lightly floured surface, roll out pie dough into a 12-inch circle. Cut into 12 rectangles, reusing scraps as needed. Place about 2 teaspoons of the strawberry mixture in the center of six dough rectangles, leaving a ½-inch border. Brush edges with water and top with remaining dough rectangles, pressing edges to seal. Generously spray tarts with cooking spray.
3. Arrange 3 tarts in a single layer in the air fryer basket and cook at 350°F for 10 minutes or until golden brown. Repeat with remaining tarts. Cool on a wire rack for about 30 minutes.
4. In a small bowl, mix powdered sugar and lemon juice until smooth. Glaze all cooled tarts with the mixture and generously top with candy sprinkles.

## NUTRITIONAL SERVING

Protein: 2.8g, Carbs: 110g, Fat: 20g, Sodium: 200mg, Sugar: 50g, Calories: ~650 kcal.

**Recipe Tips:** For a healthier twist, use whole wheat pie crust and reduce the sugar in the strawberry filling.

## 14.7 Stuffed Bagel Balls

Stuffed Bagel Balls are a delightful twist on traditional bagels, filled with creamy cheese and baked to perfection. These bite-sized treats are perfect for breakfast or as a snack, offering the classic bagel flavor in a more convenient form.

**PREPARATION TIME:** 15 minutes

**Cooking Time:** 20-25 minutes

**DIFFICULTY LEVEL:** Medium

**SERVINGS:** 2

## INGREDIENTS

59. All-purpose flour, 1 cup
60. Baking powder, 1 teaspoon
61. Salt, 1/2 teaspoon
62. Plain Greek yogurt, 1/2 cup
63. Cream cheese, 1/4 cup, softened
64. Egg, 1 large, beaten
65. Sesame seeds or poppy seeds for topping (optional)

## STEPS

1. Preheat your oven to 375°F (190°C). Line a baking sheet with parchment paper or a silicone baking mat.
2. In a medium-sized mixing bowl, combine the all-purpose flour, baking powder, and salt.
3. Add the Greek yogurt to the dry ingredients and mix until a dough forms. If the dough is too sticky, add a little more flour.
4. Divide the dough into 4 equal portions. Roll each portion into a ball.
5. Flatten each ball and place a tablespoon of softened cream cheese in the center. Carefully fold the dough around the cream cheese, sealing it completely. Roll the stuffed dough back into a ball shape.
6. Place the Stuffed Bagel Balls onto the prepared baking sheet.
7. Brush the surface of each ball with the beaten egg. If desired, sprinkle sesame seeds or poppy seeds on top.
8. Bake for 20-25 minutes or until the Stuffed Bagel Balls are golden brown. Remove from the oven and let them cool for a few minutes before serving.

66.

## NUTRITIONAL SERVING

Protein: 17g, Carbs: 48g, Fat: 12g, Sodium: 916mg, Sugar: 3g, Fiber: 2g.

 **Recipe Tips:** To enhance the bagel flavor, you can mix a pinch of garlic powder or onion powder into the dough.

## 14.8 Green Tomato BLT

Green Tomato BLT brings a delightful twist to the classic BLT sandwich. Featuring crispy fried green tomatoes and savory bacon, this recipe offers a unique blend of textures and flavors, making it a perfect choice for a satisfying lunch or casual dinner.

http://tiny.cc/afveg6

**PREPARATION TIME:** 20 minutes

Cooking Time: 5-6 minutes

**DIFFICULTY LEVEL:** Hard

**SERVINGS:** 2

### INGREDIENTS

- Green tomatoes, 10 ounces, sliced
- Salt, ½ tsp
- Pepper, ¼ tsp
- Large egg, beaten, 1
- Flour, ¼ cup
- Panko breadcrumbs, 1 cup
- Cooking spray

- Mayonnaise, ½ cup
- Green onions, diced, 2
- Freshly chopped dill, 1 tsp
- Whole wheat bread, 8 slices
- Cooked bacon, 8 strips
- Lettuce, 4 leaves, chopped

### STEPS

1. Preheat the air fryer to 350°F.
2. Slice the green tomatoes into 4 crosswise pieces each. Season with salt and pepper.
3. Set up three separate bowls with flour, beaten egg, and breadcrumbs.
4. Coat tomato slices first in flour (shaking off excess), then dip in egg, followed by breadcrumbs.
5. Place tomato slices in the air fryer basket on an oiled tray in single layers. Spray with cooking spray. Cook for 5-6 minutes or until golden brown.
6. In a separate bowl, mix mayonnaise, dill, and green onions.
7. Assemble the sandwich on four bread slices with two bacon strips, one lettuce leaf, and two tomato slices each. Spread the remaining bread slices with the mayonnaise mixture. Serve.

### NUTRITIONAL SERVING

Protein: 16g, Carb: 45g, Fat: 17g, Sodium: 2g, Sugar: 2g, Potassium: 3g, Calories: Approx. 300-350 kcal per serving.

**Recipe** **Tips:**
For extra crispiness, allow the coated tomato slices to rest for a few minutes before frying.

# Chapter 14: Substitute Ingredients Guide

## 14.1 Oreos:
Vegetarian:
- No substitutions needed.

Gluten-Free:
- Pancake: Use gluten-free pancake mix.
- Chocolate cookies: Use gluten-free chocolate cookies.

Allergen-Free:
- Chocolate cookies: Check the label for potential allergens or use allergen-free cookies.

## 14.2 Roasted Bananas:
Vegetarian:
- No substitutions needed.

Gluten-Free:
- No substitutions needed.

Allergen-Free:
- Ensure cooking spray is allergen-free.

## 14.3 Beignets:
Vegetarian:
- No substitutions needed.

Gluten-Free:
- Flour: Use gluten-free flour.

Allergen-Free:
- Ensure the butter used is allergen-free. Consider dairy-free butter for lactose intolerance.

## 14.4 House Gluten-Free Fresh Cherry Crumble:
Vegetarian:
- No substitutions needed.

Gluten-Free:
- Ensure the flour used is gluten-free (as the recipe title suggests it should be).

Allergen-Free:
- Butter: Use allergen-free or dairy-free butter.

## 14.5 Double-Glazed Air-Fried Cinnamon Biscuit Bites:
Vegetarian:
- No substitutions needed.

Gluten-Free:
- Flour: Use gluten-free flour.
- Wheat flour: Use gluten-free alternative.

Allergen-Free:
- Cold salted butter: Use allergen-free or dairy-free butter.

## 14.6 Strawberry "Pop-Tarts"
Vegetarian:
- All ingredients are already vegetarian.

Gluten-Free:
- Freeze piecrusts: Use gluten-free piecrusts. These are readily available in many supermarkets, or you can make your own using gluten-free flour.

Allergen-Free:
- Freeze piecrusts: Check the ingredient list as some may contain dairy or other allergens. If making your own, be sure to use allergen-free ingredients.
- Candy sprinkles: Some candy sprinkles can contain artificial colors, which may be allergens for some individuals. Opt for natural or allergen-free candy sprinkles.

## 14.7 Stuffed Bagel Balls
Vegetarian:
- No adjustments needed for this recipe.

Gluten-Free:
- 1 cup all-purpose flour: Use gluten-free flour blend (ensure it contains xanthan gum or a similar binding agent, or add it separately).

Allergen-Free:
- 1/2 cup plain Greek yogurt: Use dairy-free yogurt.
- 1/4 cup cream cheese: Use dairy-free cream cheese.
- 1 large egg: Use a flax egg (1 tbsp ground flaxseed mixed with 2.5 tbsp water and let sit for 5 minutes).
- Sesame seeds or poppy seeds for topping: Omit if allergic or replace with a safe topping like crushed gluten-free pretzels or allergen-free seasonings.

## 14.8 Green Tomato BLT
Vegetarian:

- Cooked pork, 8 strips: Substitute with 8 strips of vegetarian bacon (store-bought options like tempeh bacon or seitan bacon) or make your own using thinly sliced tofu marinated in a smoky sauce and then pan-fried.

Gluten-Free:
- Flour, ¼ cup: Substitute with gluten-free all-purpose flour.
- Panko breadcrumbs, 1 cup: Substitute with gluten-free breadcrumbs.
- Wheat bread, 8 slices: Substitute with gluten-free bread.

**Allergen-Free:** (Note: Always refer to allergens that are commonly known, like dairy, nuts, soy, etc. The exact allergens to be avoided would depend on individual needs.)

- Wheat bread, 8 slices: For a nut-free version, ensure gluten-free bread does not contain nut flours.
- Egg, 1: Substitute with a flax egg (1 tbsp ground flaxseed mixed with 2.5 tbsp water, let sit for 5 minutes to thicken).

When following these recommendations, it's always crucial for individuals with severe allergies or sensitivities to read product labels. Manufacturers' ingredients and processing methods can change, and cross-contamination is always a potential concern. Always consult with a doctor or nutritionist about personal dietary needs.

# Chapter 15: FAQS

How do air fryers work?

An air fryer works by circulating hot air around the food using a built-in fan. This creates a crispy, fried texture without the need for added oil. The hot air is generated by a heating element, and the temperature can be set using a thermostat or digital controls. The food is placed in a basket or tray and placed in the air fryer. The circulating hot air cooks the food quickly and evenly, resulting in a crispy exterior and tender interior. Some air fryers also have a built-in timer and automatic shut-off feature for added convenience.

What are the downsides of an air fryer?

Air fryers have some limitations and potential drawbacks to be aware of:

Capacity: Air fryers typically have a smaller capacity than traditional deep fryers, which can make them less practical for cooking large quantities of food or for larger families.

Space: Air fryers can be quite large and take up a significant amount of counter space.

Cooking time: Depending on the food being cooked and the desired level of crispiness, cooking times in an air fryer can be longer than traditional deep frying.

Temperature limitations: Air fryers typically have a lower temperature range than ovens, which can limit the types of foods that can be cooked in them.

Cleaning: Some air fryers can be difficult to clean, especially if food gets stuck in the heating element or fan.

Potential for uneven cooking: Due to the fact that food is placed in a single layer, if the food is not turned over or rearranged during the cooking process, it could lead to uneven cooking.

It's worth noting that these are not necessarily downside but are things to consider before purchasing an air fryer. Ultimately, whether an air fryer is right for you will depend on your specific cooking needs and preferences.

What is the best air fryer?

There are many different brands and models of air fryers on the market, so it can be difficult to determine the best one. Some factors to consider when choosing an air fryer include the size and capacity of the unit, the types of food you plan to cook, and your budget.

That being said, some popular and well-reviewed air fryers include:

**Philips XL Airfryer:** This large-capacity air fryer is popular for its even cooking and easy-to-use digital controls.

**Cosori Air Fryer:** This compact air fryer has a 5.8-quart capacity and includes 11 pre-set cooking options.

**Ninja Foodi:** This multi-cooker has an air fryer function but also includes pressure cooking, slow cooking, and steaming capabilities.

**GoWISE USA Air Fryer:** This air fryer features a 7-quart capacity, a digital touch screen, and 14 pre-set cooking functions.

**Cuisinart TOA-60:** This air fryer has a spacious 0.6 cubic feet of cooking space. It also has a built-in light, so you can keep an eye on your food as it cooks.

Ultimately, the best air fryer for you will depend on your specific needs and preferences. It's always recommended to read reviews and compare features before making a purchase.

What is the difference between an air fryer and an oven?

An air fryer and an oven are both kitchen appliances that can be used to cook food, but they have some key differences:

Cooking method: An air fryer cooks food by circulating hot air around it, while an oven uses heated air and radiant heat to cook food.

Cooking time: Cooking times can vary depending on the food being cooked and the desired level of doneness, but in general, food cooked in an air fryer will cook faster than food cooked in an oven.

Crispiness: An air fryer is designed to create a crispy exterior on food without the need for added oil, while an oven may not produce the same level of crispiness.

Capacity: Ovens typically have a larger capacity than air fryers and can accommodate more food at one time.

Temperature range: Air fryers typically have a lower temperature range than ovens, which can limit the types of foods that can be cooked in them.

Cooking function: Ovens typically have multiple cooking functions, such as broil, baking, roasting, and convection, while air fryers are mainly used for frying, dehydrating and roasting.

Overall, an oven is a more versatile appliance that can be used for a wider range of cooking tasks, while an air fryer is specifically designed for creating a crispy texture on food without the use of oil.


How healthy is the air fryer?

Air fryers are often marketed as a healthier alternative to traditional deep frying because they use circulating hot air to cook food instead of oil. This means that food cooked in an air fryer may contain less fat and calories than food cooked in a deep fryer.

Additionally, the cooking process of an air fryer can help to retain more of the food's nutrients since it doesn't require submerging the food in oil.

However, it's worth noting that the term "healthier" is relative as it depends on the type of food being cooked and the preparation method. For example, air-frying processed foods, such as frozen french fries, chicken nuggets, or frozen chicken tenders, may not be as healthy as cooking them in the oven, even though they are cooked with less oil.

It's also important to remember that many of the foods that are traditionally deep-fried can still be high in calories, even when cooked in an air fryer. Additionally, it's also recommended to use a minimal amount of oil, if any, when cooking with an air fryer to make the food even healthier.

In summary, cooking with an air fryer can be a healthier alternative to traditional deep frying, but the overall healthiness of the food depends on the food and preparation method.


What advantages does the air fryer have?

Air fryers have several advantages over traditional deep frying and other cooking methods:

Healthier cooking: Air fryers use hot air for cooking food, which means that food cooked in an air fryer may contain less fat and calories than food cooked in a deep fryer.

Quick and easy: Air fryers can cook food quickly and easily, and they often have digital controls and preset cooking programs that make it easy to achieve the desired level of doneness.

Convenient: Air fryers are compact, easy to use and easy to clean. They also have a built-in timer and automatic shut-off feature for added convenience.

Versatile: Air fryers can be used to cook a variety of foods such as vegetables, meats, fish, and even desserts. Some models also have a dehydrate function which allows you to make your own dried fruits, vegetables and jerky.

Crispy texture: Air fryers are designed to create a crispy exterior on food without the need for added oil, which can be particularly appealing for foods like French fries and chicken wings.

Retain nutrients: Air fryers help to retain more of the food's nutrients since it doesn't require submerging the food in oil.

It's worth noting that these advantages are based on the assumption that the food is prepared with a minimal amount of oil and that it's not deep-fried food that's high in calories, sodium, and unhealthy fats.

What not to cook in the air fryer?

While air fryers are versatile and can be used to cook a variety of foods, there are some things that you should avoid cooking in an air fryer:

Foods that are high in moisture, such as soups, stews, and casseroles, may not cook well in an air fryer.

Breaded foods: Foods that are breaded or coated with a batter may not crisp up as well in an air fryer as they do in a deep fryer, so it's best to avoid them.

Foods that are prone to sticking: Foods that are prone to sticking, such as eggs or pancakes, may not cook well in an air fryer, as the hot air may not be able to circulate around them properly.

Foods that are prone to splattering: Foods that are prone to splattering, such as bacon or ground meat, may not cook well in an air fryer, as the hot air may not be able to circulate around them properly and may make a mess.

Foods that require a lot of space: Foods that require a lot of space, such as whole chicken or turkey, may not fit in an air fryer.

Foods that are sensitive to high heat: Foods that are sensitive to high heat, such as delicate fish, may burn or cook unevenly in an air fryer.

It's always recommended to read the manual and recipes or consult the manufacturer's website to know the best way to use your air fryer and what foods are suitable for it.

How much electricity does an air fryer consume?

The amount of electricity an air fryer consumes can vary depending on the size and model of the unit, as well as the duration of use. On average, most air fryers use between 1,200 and 1,800 watts of power. This means that if you use your air fryer for an hour, it will consume between 1.2 and 1.8 kilowatt-hours (kWh) of energy.

To put that in perspective, a typical refrigerator uses around 1.2 kWh of energy per day, and a typical oven uses around 3.3 kWh per day. So an air fryer is considered to be less energy consuming than an oven but more than a refrigerator.

How much does a good air fryer cost?

The cost of an air fryer can vary widely depending on the size, brand, and features of the unit.

You can find basic models of air fryers for as low as $30 to $50, but these basic models often have a smaller capacity and less advanced features.

Mid-range models can cost between $60 and $150; these models usually have a larger capacity and more advanced features such as digital controls, multiple cooking settings, and larger cooking baskets.

High-end models can cost $150 and above; these models typically have larger capacities and more advanced features and may include additional functions such as pressure cooking or dehydrating.

It's worth noting that some well-known brands and models can be more expensive than others, but it doesn't necessarily mean that they are better. It's always important to read reviews and compare features to find the best air fryer for your needs and budget.

What is the best-selling air fryer?

It is difficult to determine the best-selling air fryer as sales figures and ranking change over time and depend on the region and market. However, some popular and well-reviewed air fryers that are considered best sellers include:

- Philips XL Airfryer
- Cosori Air Fryer
- Ninja Foodi
- GoWISE USA Air Fryer
- Cuisinart TOA-60

It's worth noting that these are some of the popular models that are considered best sellers and have a good reputation, but the best air fryer for you will depend on your specific needs and preferences. It's always recommended to read reviews and compare features before making a purchase.

What pans can you put in the air fryer?

The type of pans that can be used in an air fryer will depend on the specific model and size of the air fryer, but in general, the following types of pans are suitable for use in an air fryer:

Air fryer-specific pans: Many air fryer manufacturers sell pans that are specifically designed to fit their air fryers. These pans often have a non-stick coating and are dishwasher-safe.

Metal pans: Metal pans, such as stainless steel or aluminum, can be used in an air fryer as long as they are oven safe and fit in the fryer basket.

Ceramic pans: Ceramic pans can also be used in an air fryer as long as they are oven safe and fit in the fryer basket.

Silicone pans: Some air fryer models can accommodate silicone pans, which are often flexible, easy to clean and can be used for baking, freezing and storing food.

It's worth noting that you should avoid using pans that are not oven safe, as they may not be able to withstand the high temperatures of the air fryer and could melt or release harmful chemicals. Also, when using metal pans, it's important to ensure they are not too large or too heavy and to use oven mitts when handling them, as they can get very hot. Also, when using metal pans be sure to avoid scratching the basket of your air fryer, as it can cause damage to it.

What foods can be cooked in the air fryer?

Air fryers can be used to cook a wide variety of foods. Some popular foods that can be cooked in an air fryer include:

French fries and other fried foods: Air fryers can be used to make crispy French fries, chicken nuggets, and other fried foods with less oil than traditional deep frying.

Chicken: Air fryers can be used to cook chicken breasts, drumsticks, and wings with a crispy exterior and juicy interior.

Fish and seafood: Air fryers can be used to cook fish and seafood such as tilapia, salmon, and shrimp with a crispy exterior and moist interior.

Vegetables: Air fryers can be used to roast or dehydrate vegetables such as carrots, broccoli, and sweet potatoes with minimal oil.

Burgers and sandwiches: Air fryers can be used to cook burgers and sandwiches with a crispy exterior and juicy interior.

Desserts: Air fryers can be used to cook a variety of desserts such as cakes, cookies, and donuts with a crispy exterior and soft interior.

Tofu, tempeh and other plant-based protein can also be cooked in an air fryer.

How much does an hour of air fryer cost?
The cost of using an air fryer for an hour will depend on the wattage of the unit and the cost of electricity in your area.
On average, most air fryers use between 1,200 and 1,800 watts of power. To estimate the cost of running an air fryer for an hour, you can use the formula: (wattage of the air fryer) x (hours of use) / 1000 x (cost of electricity per kWh).
For example, if you have an air fryer that uses 1,500 watts, and your electricity rate is $0.12 per kilowatt-hour (kWh), then running your air fryer for an hour would cost you: 1,500 x 1 / 1000 x 0.12 = $0.18.

How much oil does it take in the air fryer?
The amount of oil needed to cook food in an air fryer will depend on the type of food, the desired level of crispiness and personal preference.
Air fryers use hot air for cooking food, and they are designed to create a crispy exterior on food without the need for a lot of oil. Some foods, such as French fries, chicken wings, and onion rings, can be cooked with just a small amount of oil, usually between 1 to 2 tablespoons. This amount of oil will help to create a crispy exterior, but it's not necessary.
For other foods, such as chicken breasts, fish fillets, or vegetables, you may not need to use any oil at all. The food will still cook evenly and come out crispy without added oil.
For those who prefer more oil, you can add more oil to achieve the desired level of crispiness. The key is not to overdo it, as too much oil can make the food greasy and lead to higher calorie content.

How to make bread with the air fryer?
Air fryers can be used to make bread with a crispy crust and a soft interior. Here are a few tips to help you make bread in an air fryer:
Use pre-made dough: Most air fryers are not big enough to accommodate a loaf pan, so you will want to use pre-made dough, such as store-bought frozen bread dough or homemade dough that has been shaped into a boule or round.
Preheat the air fryer: Preheat the air fryer to the desired temperature (usually around 350-375F) before placing the dough inside.
Place the dough on a tray or rack: Place the dough on a tray or rack that is sprayed with non-stick cooking spray or lined with parchment paper. This will prevent the bread from sticking to the bottom of the fryer.
Mist the dough with water: Before placing the dough in the air fryer, mist it with water. This will help create a crispy crust.
Cook the bread: Cook the bread for the recommended time and temperature in the air fryer. Check the bread for doneness by tapping the bottom of the loaf and listening for a hollow sound.
Cool and slice: Allow the bread to cool for a few minutes before slicing and serving.

How to make pizza with the air fryer?
Air fryers can be used to make pizza with a crispy crust and melted cheese. Here are a few tips to help you make pizza in an air fryer:
Use pre-made dough: You can use store-bought or homemade pizza dough. You can also use pre-made frozen pizza crusts or even flatbread or pita bread as a base.
Preheat the air fryer: Preheat the air fryer to the desired temperature (around 425F) before placing the dough inside.

Assemble the pizza: Roll out the dough to the desired thickness, and place it in a tray or rack that is sprayed with non-stick cooking spray or lined with parchment paper. Add your desired toppings, making sure not to overload the pizza, as this can cause uneven cooking.

Cook the pizza: Cook the pizza for the recommended time and temperature in the air fryer. Usually, it takes around 8-12 minutes, depending on the size of the pizza and the desired level of doneness.

Check and rotate: Check the pizza after a few minutes of cooking and rotate it if necessary to ensure even cooking.

Enjoy: Once the pizza is cooked to your liking, remove it from the air fryer and let it cool for a few minutes before slicing and serving.

How to make popcorn in the air fryer?

Air fryers can be used to make popcorn with a crispy texture and minimal oil. Here are a few tips to help you make popcorn in an air fryer:

Use popcorn kernels: You can use regular popcorn kernels and avoid using pre-popped popcorn, as it can burn and stick to the bottom of the air fryer.

Preheat the air fryer: Preheat the air fryer to the desired temperature (around 350-375F) before placing the kernels inside.

Add the kernels: Add the kernels to the fryer basket or tray. You can add a small amount of oil if desired, but it's unnecessary.

Cook the popcorn: Cook the popcorn for the recommended time in the air fryer. Usually, it takes around 3-5 minutes for the kernels to start popping.

Shake the air fryer: Shake the air fryer occasionally to ensure that the popcorn pops evenly.

Enjoy: Once the popcorn is done, remove it from the air fryer and let it cool for a few minutes before adding any seasoning or butter if you prefer.

# Chapter 16: 30-Day Meal Plan

| Day | Breakfast | Lunch | Snack | Dinner |
|---|---|---|---|---|
| 1 | French Toast Sticks, p.20 | Crispy Air Fryer Eggplant Parmesan, p.37 | Zesty Tofu Sriracha Spring Rolls, p.28 | Sweet and Sour Pineapple Pork, p.49 |
| 2 | Toad in the Hole Tarts, p.20 | Roasted Brussels Sprouts With Balsamic, p.38 | Fiesta Chicken Fingers, p.29 | Spicy Chicken Breasts, p.49 |
| 3 | Churros, p.21 | Chicken Nuggets, p.39 | Cheeseburger Onion Rings, p.30 | Reuben Calzones, p.50 |
| 4 | Hard Boiled Eggs, p.22 | Baked Apples, p.39 | Garlic Rosemary Sprouts, p.31 | Steak with Garlic Herb Butter, p.50 |
| 5 | Omelet, p.22 | Dumplings, p.40 | Ravioli, p.31 | Fried Rice with Sesame Sriracha Sauce, p.51 |
| 6 | Air Fryer Egg McMuffin, p.23 | Pork Special Chops, p.40 | Taquitos, p.32 | Roast Chicken, p.52 |
| 7 | Breakfast Pizza, p.24 | Chicken Chimichangas, p.41 | General Tso's Cauliflower, p.32 | Mini Swedish Meatballs, p.52 |
| 8 | Cherry and Cream Cheese Danish, p.24 | Simple Chicken Burrito Bowls, p.42 | Nashville Hot Chicken, p.33 | Za'atar Lamb Chops, p.53 |
| 9 | Southern Cheese, p.25 | Chicken Soft Tacos, p.43 | Pumpkin Fries, p.34 | Meatballs, p.54 |
| 10 | Apple Fritters, p.19 | Pork Schnitzel, p.43 | Pickles, p.28 | Tostones (Twice Air-Fried Plantains), p.54 |
| 11 | French Toast Sticks, p.20 | Crispy Air Fryer Eggplant Parmesan, p.37 | Zesty Tofu Sriracha Spring Rolls, p.28 | Sweet and Sour Pineapple Pork, p.49 |
| 12 | Toad in the Hole Tarts, p.20 | Roasted Brussels Sprouts With Balsamic, p.38 | Fiesta Chicken Fingers, p.29 | Spicy Chicken Breasts, p.49 |
| 13 | Churros, p.21 | Chicken Nuggets, p.39 | Cheeseburger Onion Rings, p.30 | Reuben Calzones, p.50 |
| 14 | Hard Boiled Eggs, p.22 | Baked Apples, p.39 | Garlic Rosemary Sprouts, p.31 | Steak with Garlic Herb Butter, p.50 |
| 15 | Omelet, p.22 | Dumplings, p.40 | Ravioli, p.31 | Fried Rice with Sesame Sriracha Sauce, p.51 |
| 16 | Air Fryer Egg McMuffin, p.23 | Pork Special Chops, p.40 | Taquitos, p.32 | Roast Chicken, p.52 |

| Day | Breakfast | Lunch | Snack | Dinner |
|---|---|---|---|---|
| 17 | Breakfast Pizza, p.24 | Chicken Chimichangas, p.41 | General Tso's Cauliflower, p.32 | Mini Swedish Meatballs, p.52 |
| 18 | Cherry and Cream Cheese Danish, p.24 | Simple Chicken Burrito Bowls, p.42 | Nashville Hot Chicken, p.33 | Za'atar Lamb Chops, p.53 |
| 19 | Southern Cheese, p.25 | Chicken Soft Tacos, p.43 | Pumpkin Fries, p.34 | Meatballs, p.54 |
| 20 | Apple Fritters, p.19 | Pork Schnitzel, p.43 | Pickles, p.28 | Tostones, p.54 |
| 21 | French Toast Sticks, p.20 | Crispy Air Fryer Eggplant Parmesan, p.37 | Zesty Tofu Sriracha Spring Rolls, p.28 | Sweet and Sour Pineapple Pork, p.49 |
| 22 | Toad in the Hole Tarts, p.20 | Roasted Brussels Sprouts With Balsamic, p.38 | Fiesta Chicken Fingers, p.29 | Spicy Chicken Breasts, p.49 |
| 23 | Churros, p.21 | Chicken Nuggets, p.39 | Cheeseburger Onion Rings, p.30 | Reuben Calzones, p.50 |
| 24 | Hard Boiled Eggs, p.22 | Baked Apples, p.39 | Garlic Rosemary Sprouts, p.31 | Steak with Garlic Herb Butter, p.50 |
| 25 | Omelet, p.22 | Dumplings, p.40 | Ravioli, p.31 | Fried Rice with Sesame Sriracha Sauce, p.51 |
| 26 | Air Fryer Egg McMuffin, p.23 | Pork Special Chops, p.40 | Taquitos, p.32 | Roast Chicken, p.52 |
| 27 | Breakfast Pizza, p.24 | Chicken Chimichangas, p.41 | General Tso's Cauliflower, p.32 | Mini Swedish Meatballs, p.52 |
| 28 | Cherry and Cream Cheese Danish, p.24 | Simple Chicken Burrito Bowls, p.42 | Nashville Hot Chicken, p.33 | Za'atar Lamb Chops, p.53 |
| 29 | Southern Cheese, p.25 | Chicken Soft Tacos, p.43 | Pumpkin Fries, p.34 | Meatballs, p.54 |
| 30 | Apple Fritters, p.19 | Pork Schnitzel, p.43 | Pickles, p.28 | Tostones, p.54 |

# Conversion Tables

Liquid Conversion Table

| Measure | Fluid OZ | TBSP | tsp | Liter (l) Milliliter (ml) |
|---------|----------|------|-----|---------------------------|
| 1 gallon | 4 quarts | 256 tbsp | 768 tsp | 3.1 l |
| 4 cups | 1 quart | 64 tbsp | 192 tsp | 0.95 l |
| 2 cups | 1 pint | 32 tbsp | 96 tsp | 470 ml |
| 1 cup | 8 oz | 16 tbsp | 48 tsp | 237 ml |
| 3/4 cup | 6 oz | 12 tbsp | 36 tsp | 177 ml |
| 2/3 cup | 5 oz | 11 tbsp | 32 tsp | 158 ml |
| 1/2 cup | 4 oz | 8 tbsp | 24 tsp | 118 ml |
| 1/3 cup | 3 oz | 5 tbsp | 16 tsp | 79 ml |
| 1/4 cup | 2 oz | 4 tbsp | 12 tsp | 59 ml |
| 1/8 cup | 1 oz | 2 tbsp | 6 tsp | 30 ml |
| 1/16 cup | 0.5 oz | 1 tbsp | 3 tsp | 15 ml |

Solid Conversion Table

| Imperial | Metric |
|----------|--------|
| 1/2 oz. | 14 g |
| 1 oz. | 28 g |
| 2 oz. | 57 g |
| 3 oz. | 85 g |
| 4 oz. | 113 g |
| 5 oz. | 142 g |
| 6 oz. | 170 g |
| 7 oz. | 199 g |
| 8 oz. | 227 g |
| 9 oz. | 255 g |
| 10 oz. | 284 g |
| 12 oz | 340 g |
| 1 lb. | 454 g |
| 1 ½ lb. | 680 g |
| 2 lb. | 907 g |
| 2.2 lb. | 1 kg |

# Authors' Note

Dear Reader,

Thank you for choosing to read **"The 15-Minute Air Fryer Cookbook for Beginners"** We hope that you have enjoyed reading through the book and have learned some valuable information about air frying.

Air frying is a great way to cook food quickly and easily without having to worry about the mess and hassle of deep frying. It's a healthier alternative to traditional frying methods, and it's perfect for people who are looking to eat healthier or lose weight.

In this book, we have included a wide variety of easy-to-follow recipes that are perfect for beginners. We have also included essential tips and tricks to help you master the art of air frying.

We would be extremely grateful and joyful if you could give an honest review on Amazon.

**Your feedback is important to us**, and it helps us to improve our books and make them even better for our readers.

Thank you again for choosing to read " **The 15-Minute Air Fryer Cookbook for Beginners**" We hope that you have enjoyed it and that it has helped you to become an expert in air frying.

Scan the Qr code with the camera of your mobile phone, click on the link that opens and you can leave your review. Thank you.

# https://bit.ly/airfryerkindlerev

# Conclusion

In conclusion, this air fryer cookbook is a valuable resource for anyone who wants to take advantage of the many benefits of cooking with an air fryer. This cookbook provides a wide variety of delicious and healthy recipes that are easy to prepare and offer a great way to explore the world of air frying.

This air fryer cookbook typically includes recipes for breakfast, lunch, dinner, and even desserts that are suitable for all tastes and dietary preferences. From crispy French fries to juicy chicken breasts, from crunchy vegetables to mouthwatering desserts, you'll find a wide variety of dishes that can be made with your air fryer.

The cookbook also provides tips and techniques for getting the most out of your air fryer, including how to choose the right model, how to clean and maintain it, and how to troubleshoot common problems. It also includes information on how to cook with less oil and how to make your favorite meals healthier and more delicious.

Overall, this air fryer cookbook is an essential tool for anyone who wants to explore the world of air frying and discover the many benefits of this innovative cooking method. It will help you take full advantage of your air fryer and enjoy delicious meals every day.

# Recipes Index

Made in the USA
Las Vegas, NV
19 April 2024